It's Time To Come Out Of Lo-debar

It's Time To
COME OUT OF
LO-DEBAR

Fidel M. Donaldson

"The Lord is my shepherd; I shall not want. He maketh me to lie down in green pastures: he leadeth me beside the still waters: He restoreth my soul."
Psalm 23:1-2

Fidel M. Donaldson

It's Time To Come Out Of Lo-debar

Scripture quotations are from the King James Version of the Bible unless otherwise stated. Hebrew and Greek definitions are taken from Strong's Exhaustive Concordance.

ISBN: 9780982771051
LCCN: 2014957768

Printed in the United States of America

FOREWORD

Have you spent the majority of your life living in the pit? Do you have dreams and visions of living a fulfilled life, full of vitality and adventure? Are you simply sick and tired and tired of being sick and tired, of experiencing life from the bottom? You have the right book at the right time. This is your ordained season to confront and break free from the low places in your life that has kept you in the darkness; Lo-debar. Apostle Fidel Donaldson has impacted the lives of many across the world through his passionate, revelatory preaching of the Gospel of Jesus Christ—bringing salvation, healing and deliverance to many. This book is no exception—to all those who are open and ready for complete change. Not only is Lo-debar explained and exposed but steps on how to come out of this dry, dark place are revealed in a practical way.

This book is not a quick, temporary fix but it holds the revelation that will lead you to your divine deliverance from your pain and set you in the place to manifest and fulfill your destiny. Once your deliverance has come, remember my friend to go and help someone else. Truth is, this is your time to come out of Lo-debar and experience the love of God in a way you've never experienced it before.

Your life is changing now!

Karliss Quisenberry

ACKNOWLEDGEMENTS

Dedicated to King Jesus: The Good Shepherd!

My heartfelt thanks and gratitude go out to Dr. Shirley Inniss, Karliss Quisenberry and Anita Choate for the hours spent proof reading and editing the manuscript. To Emmanuel Haniah and Nicole Sabrina Barnes-Broderick for their transparency in sharing their personal stories. To my childhood friend Leslie Minto for the many acts of kindness shown to me. To the Eagles from The Fourth Watch, The Hour Of Power and The Chain Breakers Prayer Lines. God bless my brother Patrice F. Donaldson and all Christian Soldiers who refuse to stay in Lo-debar. To my wife for life Lady Paulette Donaldson and all our wonderful, unique and creative children, I say Agape Shalom!

Cover Design & Layout by D'edge Media, LLC / dedgemedia.com

INTRODUCTION

At one time or another we've all found ourselves in a place of depression and despair. Decisions we made or the irresponsibility of others in the way they handled or mishandled us caused severe emotional pain and trauma which affected our walk with the Lord and our interaction with others. At five years old Mephibosheth was dropped by his nurse when she made a decision to flee hastily based on news she received that his grandfather and father were killed on the battle field. She made an assumption that his life was in danger—and that assumption caused her to take a course of action which became very detrimental to him. Her decision caused him to become lame in both feet—plunging him into a low place of depression and despair, a place called Lo-debar. The term Lo-debar will be used interchangeably to represent both a physical and a mental state. Lo-debar means no pasture, it is a dry place.

How should we react when we are the recipient of tragic news like the death of a loved one, a diagnosis of cancer or some other life threatening disease? The decision or decisions we make and the action we take will have a far reaching and long lasting effect on us, both emotionally and physically. Mcphibosheth spent years in Lo-debar, lame in his feet and lame in his emotions. He was oblivious to the fact there was a king who had made an oath with his dad to bless his offspring. The God of heaven made an oath with Abraham to bless all the families of the earth through him. The blessing became available when God's only begotten Son Jesus was birthed into the earth as a King, with a mandate to rescue those whose lives are marred and scarred through the crippling effects of being dropped.

The purpose of this book is to encourage and exhort the reader to know that Lo-debar should not be a dwelling place. Uncontrollable circumstances can land us in that place but we must remember—there is no tragedy so egregious that the Lord cannot deliver you from its effect. Many have perished in Lo-debar because they were totally consumed by the darkness of the low place. You may come to a place where you feel you don't have the strength to journey out of Lo-debar but do not give up because you were created to be more than a conqueror through Jesus Christ who loves you.

CONTENTS

PART 1:

FAITH COMETH BY HEARING: BUT DOUBT DOES ALSO

Chapter 1

—■—

Hearing

Hearing is one of the five senses and represents a very important principle or concept in the Scriptures. Deuteronomy 6:4 records a Jewish prayer called the Shema. The prayer begins with the word Hear. It is the centerpiece of the prayers prayed by many Jewish people in the morning and in the evening. It is considered by observant Jews to be the most important part of their prayer service. It is very obvious why the prayer begins with the word hear. If our prayers are not heard then we are praying in vain. If our prayers are heard and answered by God but we are unable to hear His answer, our situation will not change. Hearing is vitally important but so is taking the proper course of action based on what we hear.

According to the scriptures, faith, the thing that pleases God comes by hearing and by hearing His word. If we are to be victorious in our walk with God, it is incumbent upon us to make sure we are able to hear and obey Him. We must guard our ear-gate to ensure our hearing continues to be acute. A look at the natural ear can give us great insight into how we can be more effective in hearing what is being spoken by God.

Natural and Spiritual Ear

In the manner in which the natural ear is responsible for detecting sound and is responsible for balance and positioning of the body—the inner or what I call the spiritual ear is responsible for detecting the sound from the Holy Spirit to give balance and positioning to the body of Christ. This is why we-must be careful how you process and respond to what you hear—both in the natural and in the realm of the spirit.

Balance, motion and hearing takes place in the inner ear. The outer ear receives sound waves then transmits them to the middle ear where they are modulated and sent to a nerve in the inner ear. The nerve sends the information to the temporal lobe of the brain where it is processed as sound. The brain's role in hearing is very important—it translates impulses from the ear into sounds we can understand. Without the translation from the brain the sounds you hear would be unintelligible. When the ear receives the sound it is like raw data but it becomes intelligible when the brain processes it. I think it is safe to say that hearing takes place in the brain not in the ear—this is important to know because thought precedes action and our thoughts are affected by the things we hear and the things we hear will affect our movements for better or for worse. When we hear the word of God and act by faith the ensuing results will be beneficial to us. When we hear bad news and allow doubt and fear to invade our minds the ensuing results will affect us negatively. The positive or negative effects of what you hear and your subsequent response and reaction will not be limited to you but will affect the people you are connected to.

There is a story recorded in *1 Samuel Chapter 4* of the reaction of the Priest Eli when he heard that the Philistines had captured the Ark of the Covenant. Eli was ninety-eight years old and his eyes were dim but his hearing was intact. I have heard that individuals who are blind develop an acute sense of hearing in order to compensate for their loss of sight. When you can't see your way out of a negative situation—be still in God's presence and listen for His instructions.

The Israelites in Shiloh cried out when they were given the news the Ark was captured. When Eli heard the noise he inquired about the reason for the tumult. He was told by a man out of the army of Benjamin that Israel fled before the Philistines. There was a great slaughter of the people; Eli's two sons Hophni and Phinehas were dead and the ark was taken. When Eli heard the news, he fell off his seat backwards and broke his neck. When God's presence is not felt in your life and His guidance and direction is clearly absent, your steps will falter. The ensuing result will be the loss of your surefootedness and your balance. This loss will cause you to plummet to the ground in a posture of uncertainty and fear—the ground that was once firm and rock solid under your feet now feels as if it is giving way and you are slowly sinking.

Eli had a daughter-in-law who was the wife of his son Hophni — she was pregnant at the time she received the news and was near delivery. When she heard that the Ark was taken and her father-in-law and her husband were dead, she began to travail as labor pains came upon her. As she was at the point of death the midwives around her tried to console her by telling her not to fear because she was going to have a son but she did not respond to them. She named the child Ichabod because she said the glory of God had departed from Israel. The tragic loss left her feeling hopeless and she transferred that sense of hopelessness to her child by giving him the name Ichabod. You will face immense tragedies in your life but never lose hope and place your trust in Jesus because He is able to deliver. As terrible as the situation may have been, she should have hoped for a better and brighter tomorrow because weeping may endure for a night but joy, blissful, unspeakable, exuberant joy arrives at the crack of dawn, at the break of day *(Psalm 30:5)*.

With God there is always hope in the new dawn, always hope on the horizon because our hope, our trust, our shield, the keeper of us all is the Lord, The Lord is thy keeper: the Lord is thy shade upon thy right hand *(Psalm 121:5)*. Every single day that the Lord brings, you must welcome with glad tidings; you must embrace it with gratitude despite what the day may bring forth because another day of life in the Lord is truly a precious gift. The very word of God declares, This is the day which the LORD hath made; we will rejoice and be glad in it *(Psalm 118:24)*.

As soon as God rolls back the heavy curtain of the previous somber night, He gives the command for His sun to rise. The mountains melt and quake, the trees of the forest sing for joy, the flowers of the field bloom in loveliness, the wind blows the trumpet for all of God's creation to stand at attention honoring Him in a spirit of exaltation and appreciation for bringing forth yet another day; From the rising of the sun to its setting, the name of the Lord is to be praised *(Psalm 113:3 ESV)*! Basking in the proverbial warmth of God's radiance, we can confidently and assuredly dry all the tears shed throughout the night.

We find ourselves embarking on a new morning, with a fresh new start, with a totally new perspective and a new expectation immersed in optimism for a new miracle from our God who says in His word, For with God nothing shall be impossible *(Luke 1:37)*. Oh the impossibility, the implausibility, the improbability, the immutability of God!   For I am the LORD, I change not *(Malachi 3:6)*. God's face is shining brilliantly upon us and our hearts are lifted; our spirits are lifted; our burdens are lifted.

There are many people who have impulsively and tragically committed suicide after receiving catastrophic news. Many have taken a course of action thoughtlessly and carelessly based on what they have heard which had dire consequences for years to come. Mephibosheth did not commit suicide but when he encountered King David he described himself as a dead dog.

The King Is Dead—Long Live the King

Mephibosheth was a direct member of a royal family; the grandson of a king and the son of a prince. The action taken by his nurse based on news she heard—had a rippling and crippling effect on him. His grandfather and his father were killed on the battlefield. After the death of his grandfather Saul and his father Jonathan, David was crowned king.   It was a time of rejoicing but also a time of great bloodshed. Abner the captain over Saul's army took Saul's son Ish-bosheth and attempted to make him king over all Israel but he was not God's choice. A civil war broke out between David's men and the house of Saul.

Fleeing when no one is Chasing

Mephibosheth was five years old when his nurse received the news that his grandfather and father were killed. She assumed Mephibosheth would be killed because of his connection to the previous king and prince; her assumption provoked by fear and terror redefined and interrupted his life for years to come. Tragic news is not something that is easy to handle so we must be extremely careful not to worsen an already bad situation with actions that are taken out of a mind responding in panic.

How we process tragic news can make all the difference between our living and our dying. For instance—if an individual receives tragic news that a cancerous growth is found in their body, the course of action taken can be the deciding and final factor as to whether they will extend their life or shorten it. Instead of operating and making decisions out of a place of fear, that individual should clear their mind of doom and gloom and get into a quiet place where they can pray and seek the counsel of God. Once the diagnosis is made there should not be an automatic assumption made that radiation and chemotherapy is the only way for survival. A determination should be made through discernment and the advice of multiple doctors as to what is the best course of action to treat the illness. The first doctor to be consulted should be Doctor Jesus because He took stripes on His body for your healing. A radical change in diet and nutrition may be the answer and not an invasive treatment with radioactive chemicals. I lost a dear friend by the name of Yvonne Ross to cancer and had the honor of doing her eulogy. I vividly remember her telling me on one occasion how she was given the wrong dose during treatment. I thank God for the wisdom He has given men and women but we must always remember, they practice medicine but the Lord Jesus has perfected healing.

Who is Watching Your Baby?

When a woman conceives and carries her baby to term, she will go through months of dealing with changes in her body. She has to deal with intense labor pains from the contractions which facilitate the turning of the baby and its downward movement through the birth canal. Once her baby is born she forgets about the pain as her soul is filled with joy at the sight of her child. Some mothers have experienced a short-lived joy as their baby was stolen by some individual pretending to be a nurse. There have been documented instances of babysitters abusing the babies they were to care for and protect. How many times have you heard stories of babies dying from head trauma due to shaken baby syndrome? The baby was violently shaken by the caretaker because he or she would not stop crying. Whether your baby is a natural baby or a vision in the first stages of gestational development that was given to you by the Lord, you must be very careful and guarded in who you allow to handle it.

Mephibosheth's nurse may have been a wonderful caretaker up to that point but one decision made in haste can lead to terrible consequences. At five years old he was totally dependent on her for care. She made a decision based on the news to pick him up and flee hastily. Her rash decision caused him to fall and become lame in his feet—as the story develops we will see that the negative effect on his walk also had a terrible effect on his self-worth. All these things were caused by the nurse's fear of the bad tidings she received. Her intentions may have been good but good intentions don't always produce good results. Actions taken based on fear from some tragic news will often produce an undesired outcome. When news of a tragic situation reaches us we should endeavor to operate from a calm spirit not from the spirit of fear. It is not easy to remain calm and rational when dealing with a tragic situation but we must endeavor to do so by putting our faith and trust in God implicitly. Hasty actions will create additional problems so it is better to remain calm and trust the Holy Spirit to lead and guide. Once you are able to tune out the voices of fear and doubt, you will be able to hear what the Spirit of truth is saying. The Holy Spirit is the Spirit of truth.

Chapter 2

---∎---

The Fear Factor

Faith and fear are akin to light and darkness; they are diametrically opposed to each other because they cannot dwell in the same place simultaneously. Faith from God's word and trust in His word produces light which allows us to see spiritually and naturally; fear from a negative contrary word brings darkness which blocks our vision both spiritually and naturally. In Psalm 119:105 David wrote, Thy word is a lamp unto my feet, and a light unto my path—He went on to say the entrance of God's word brings light. The word has to be mixed with faith in order to get the desired results. There are some in the body of Christ who hear great preaching and teaching but still operate out of a spirit of fear because the preaching and teaching of the word is not acted upon with complete faith. They tremble in fear and quickly cower in retreat when entering into enemy territory instead of preparing, mobilizing and defending themselves armed with the word of God.

When they operate in a spirit of fear, it stunts their faith and trust in God. Like Mephibosheth, It causes their walk with God to become laborious, hampered, and disabled. They become lame, spiritually weakened and emotionally impaired; with a life plagued by missteps and mishaps resulting in misdirection as they meander and stumble about foolishly and quite aimlessly. They miss hearing from God because of fear; feelings of fear are a major contradiction that conflicts with the very word of God eluding and denying access to the abundant life promised to you by Jesus.

What faith is to God fear is to the devil. It is impossible to please God without faith. Having fear is repellant to God, it is abhorrent to Him and the enemy is pleased when we operate in the spirit of fear.

The God-kind of faith comes one way and one way only, by hearing and by hearing the word of God! Once a negative word is received, it must be counteracted and denounced by a word from God. Failing to do so will cause you great harm and those negative words will now be internalized and deeply imbedded in your spirit.

When Job received tragic news that his livestock of animals and his children were wiped out by a series of tragic events—his response was, *"For the thing which I greatly feared is come upon me, and that which I was afraid of is come unto me" Job 3:25*. I truly believe fear opens a door for the enemy to operate in our lives. The Bible describes Job as a man who was perfect and upright, one who feared God and eschewed evil. He is described as the greatest of all the men of the east and that is a great distinction to hold. Tragedy will reveal certain things about you; as great a man as he was, he greatly feared certain things. The greatest and most courageous people may put up a front displaying false bravado while inherently they harbor certain weaknesses. To his credit, when everything was falling apart around Job and his wife questioned why he did not curse God and die—he continued to bless the name of Lord.

When you are able to bless the name of the Lord in the midst of your tragedy, you will receive the instructions from Him necessary to address and alleviate the problem. Deliverance may take some time but hold fast to your integrity like Job, deliverance and restoration will surely come.

About Face

When King Hezekiah was sick unto death the Prophet Isaiah was sent to him to inform him to get his house in order because he would die and not live. The news was tragic for Hezekiah but he did not act impulsively. The Bible describes his posture this way, *"Then he turned his face to the wall, and prayed unto the Lord, saying, I beseech thee, O Lord, remember now how I have walked before thee in truth and with a perfect heart, and have done that which is good in thy sight. And Hezekiah wept sore" 2 Kings 20:2-3*. By the time the Prophet Isaiah reached the middle court of the palace, God sent him back to the king with good news.

What if Hezekiah had reacted in the flesh when he first received the news? I believe he would have missed his opportunity to receive the good news from the mouth of the prophet. When he focused on God in the tragedy, he began to petition God pleading for his life by bringing forth the record of good deeds he had accomplished during his life. God heard him and sent Isaiah back to tell him He was adding fifteen years to his life. Had Hezekiah received the devastating news of his impending death in quiet resignation and acceptance, God would have followed through with His word that he was to die at the appointed time; Hezekiah was not ready to die and fought for his life by crying out to God.

When your soul cries in agony for the living God, when you fervently seek the face of the Father in desperation, when you know you have no one else on this earth you can turn to; your plaintive cry will penetrate heaven, piercing the very heart of God who sits on the throne of grace and mercy. God will hear and act on your behalf to deliver you. Having a close relationship with God entitles His children to certain rights; one is the right to be heard. *Psalm 145:18-20 NKJV* verifies this, The LORD is near to all who call upon Him, To all who call upon Him in truth. He will fulfill the desire of those who fear Him; He also will hear their cry and save them. The LORD preserves all who love Him, But all the wicked He will destroy.

I believe God will allow a negative situation to come our way to teach us to trust in Him exclusively in every circumstance. The nurse's supposition caused her to be hasty while trying to escape with Mephibosheth. It was not uncommon during those times for the offspring of the previous king to be killed by someone acting on behalf of the new king who felt he may be a threat to the new monarch. When Saul and Jonathan were killed—the new king was David and he was a man after God's heart, besides, Mephibosheth's father Jonathan had made a covenant with David and it was a covenant that would surely spare his life. The covenant meant that each person would take care of the other's family in the event that one died. The nurse may not have been privy to the covenant and she may not have known that David was the one anointed by God to be the next king. It is interesting to note that the news she received of Saul and Jonathan's death came out of Jezreel and Jezreel means, God scatters.

The bad news out of Jezreel caused Mephibosheth's nurse to scatter hastily. God had taken the kingdom from Saul because of his disobedience so the battle against the Philistines was not favorable to him causing his death and the death of his son Jonathan.

Mephibosheth was the son of Jonathan but he would not be the next king because God chose David. When God choses an individual there is isn't anything others can do to circumvent His choice. You were chosen by and connected to the King of kings and the Lord of lords. Your connection to Him means you do not have to panic in times of trouble; it means you can have peace in the midst of the storm. Your connection to Jesus means He is in control and when He is in control the situation will not get out of control. Jesus is the author and finisher of our faith Hebrews 12:2. We must seek Him in prayer for His will to be done no matter the severity of the situation. Always look for the Christ in the crisis. Only in Jesus can we find fulfillment, wholeness, and completeness in every area of our lives when we follow the will of God. Because of his nurse's misstep impelled by fear, Mephibosheth was made incomplete and imperfect suffering from a major deformity in both feet that would restrict his mobility and his ability to stand on his own. His lack of physical mobility adversely affected his mental mobility, causing him to be dependent on others.

Chapter 3

— ■ —

Who Dropped You?

Who dropped you? Who mishandled and immobilized you? Who caused you to stumble, slip and suffer a major fall that you could not recover from, losing your balance along with the ability to stand on your own feet? Who tripped you or rather who tripped you up? What impediment caused you to lose your footing and break your stride halting your steps? Who is the responsible party and was it done out of malice or was it done out of ignorance? Who persecuted you? Who weakened you? Who bullied you? Who abused you? Who abandoned you? Who denied you? Who despised you? Who rejected you? Who incapacitated you ruthlessly marking you for life and setting you up for misery and failure by thwarting and overthrowing the good plans, the divine plans, the foreordained plans and destiny that God devised for your life? What caused you to become permanently lame in your feet—compelling you to never look up, to never look above or beyond your very real or imagined disabilities and perceived inferiorities—creating a stumbling block, a deterrent which caused an impasse in your walk in life that obscured and distorted your true identity of just who God created you to be?

Who was it that made your straight pathway in life pathetically crooked? Who irreparably scarred you and who massively wounded you by arresting your development for a bright, unencumbered future, sending you into a downward spiral and denying you the privilege to attain greater heights of success and to ascend the ladder to grander levels of accomplishments and status? What devastating and traumatizing event produced a crutch—a severe crippling, debilitating effect impacting, impairing and disturbing your emotions?

If only you had not been dropped, if only you had not suffered a fall, if only you were complete and whole, if only you had not been irreparably damaged how very different the outcome of your life would have been. If only they had loved you, wanted you, supported you, protected you, defended you and shielded you. If only they had comforted you and cradled you, holding you tightly and securely with tenderness and kindness never letting go. If only they had carefully and lovingly watched over you preventing the full impact of your fall to inevitable destruction.

Instead they chose to perform their dastardly deed of intentionally and hastily dropping you and handicapping you. In one fleeting moment, in a rapid blink of an eye all is lost and spoiled, shattered and ruined; everything has come crashing to the ground upending and fracturing in pieces your hopes, dreams, visions and future but most importantly the very quality of your life. Your most ardent desires are now dashed and fragmented, sending you down a dusty and desolate road to Lo-debar instead of a land flowing richly with God's blessings.

Was it a husband or a wife whom you trusted with your entire heart, your mind, your body and your soul? They took your best years, took your love, commitment and your dedication then suddenly and brutally dropped you through divorce or abandonment as soon as they thought the grass was greener on the other side. On the other side they thought they found someone who could do better than you but they failed miserably in their decision to leave because they based their judgment solely on the outward adorning, not on true discernment. They were willing to break up the family, leaving you and the children traumatized so they could fulfill some unrealistic fantasy.

A properly functioning family unit is an integral part of any society. When I use the term family unit, I am referring to the family as it is described in the word of God— *"Therefore shall a man leave his father and his mother, and shall cleave unto his wife: and they shall be one flesh" Genesis 2:24.* How ironic that the very next chapter of Genesis, chapter three, introduces us to the serpent.

Who Dropped You?

The serpent wants to come in and cause separation and divorce by tempting and convincing the husband to drop the wife or the wife to drop the husband which results in their dropping their children and in turn their children dropping their own children and the cycle and behavior of dropping our loved ones is established and perpetuated for generations to come. The serpent is not described as being more subtle than any beast of the field for nothing. He will manifest as an angel of light in order to gain entrance and access to our souls to deceive us into going against the word of God so that we feel justified in dropping Him and in turn we feel God is forced to ultimately drop us but God refuses to be dropped not wanting one of His children to fall by the wayside discarded and displaced.

Were you dropped by a husband who woke up one day after many years of marriage to tell you he no longer wanted to be married to you? He left you shocked and traumatized because there were no apparent warning signs. The news blindsided you and left you emotionally and financially crippled and unstable. Your whole life was turned upside down because of the selfish act of one individual—an individual whose thought process was not governed by a family first creed. Hindsight is 20/20 and with time you began to realize there were warning signs that you chose to ignore.

Dropped by his nurse, Mephibosheth had a man named Machir who voluntarily chose to carry him and bring him into his household perhaps out of pity or some sense of obligation. Once dropped, who had to pick up the pieces and carry you? Who was forced to carry you throughout the duration of your life fostering a precedence of dependence and reliance on others? There are individuals who skillfully and strategically use being dropped as a rite of passage and privilege to gain entitlement; they make unrealistic, heavy demands fully expecting others to carry them through life even when they are mature, fully grown and capable adults. They use the misfortune of having been dropped by someone who disabled and disfigured them as a viable crutch and perfect opportunity to shun all sense of culpability for their own life. They make lame excuse after lame excuse for their behavior crying out in a constant fit of despair and anguish, wallowing in a world of self-pity and neediness filled with unfairness for having been dropped and cast aside.

13

With the fall of humanity through Adam all of us were dropped but Jesus died and has risen from the grave so we can have the fortitude to rise from the low place. Jesus is the good Shepherd to His flock, He picks us up and sets us back on course when we have fallen or when we have been dropped. Lean on King Jesus because He is the Master Restorer. Bow down and worship King Jesus because He is the Master Redeemer. When you give King Jesus mastery and sovereignty to be the Lord of your life, when you make a solemn pledge of fidelity and vow your humble allegiance to Him, when your heart beats as one with Him in integrity, passion and adoration, it is in that moment of spiritual coupling that negative things from your former life ceases to exist. *Luke 5:11 says, And when they had brought their ships to land, they forsook all, and followed him; and in Luke 5:27-28,* And after these things he went forth, and saw a publican, named Levi, sitting at the receipt of custom: and he said unto him, Follow me. And he left all, rose up, and followed Him. In our commitment to follow and walk with Jesus we must forsake all, we must abandon all, we must drop everything in our lives to embark on a new journey leaving our past behind.

With heartfelt tenderness and loving compassion Jesus is the one who will gently lift us up, He is the one who will set us aright, He is the one that will gird us up. Allow Jesus to save you, comfort you and assist you. Jesus will instill hope and confidence in you to the supreme degree. He will empower and encourage you not only to walk on your own two feet but to soar to majestic heights expanding your wings to soar higher and higher. *Jesus said to the man who was an invalid who suffered with an infirmity for thirty-eight years, Rise, take up thy bed, and walk John 5:8.* Whatever has made you take flight in haste causing you to slip and fall, whatever has made you lame, whatever has made you spiritually, physically, mentally and emotionally ill, Jesus is ready to raise you up and heal you because He is the resurrection and the life.

Jesus declared, I am the resurrection, and the life: he that believeth in me, though he were dead, yet shall he live John 11:25. Do not live a life of defeat taking life lying down acting like an invalid but seize the opportunity to rise up. Take up your bed and arise from your affliction, your bed of heartache, despondency, lameness and indolence.

Rise up out of the low place, rise up out of Lo-debar, rise up out of the land of desolation and deadness and walk with the King! It is entirely your choice to stay in the land of Lo-debar languishing in your bed of affliction or rise to the occasion and become the person God has created you to be. Your focus should not be on the situation or the person that caused it. Your reliance, your attention, and your deepest love have to be centered on Jesus.

Jesus is the one who will gently lift us up, He is the one who will set us aright, He is the one who will gird us up. Allow Jesus to save you, comfort you and assist you. Jesus said in *Matthew 16:24-25, If any man will come after me, let him deny himself, and take up his cross, and follow me. For whosoever will save his life shall lose it: and whosoever will lose his life for my sake shall find it.* You must be willing to die to self in order to live exclusively for Jesus. Dying to self will require opening your eyes to the truth found in God's word; it will require you to stop blaming others by taking responsibility for your life and casting aside all the useless crutches that deliberately sabotage you in order break free from the confines of disempowerment and never-ending excuses.

In our resurrection and new life we will have our feet planted solidly on the ground walking in the liberality and freedom of the vocation in which we have all been called under the care, instruction and guidance of our good Shepherd. *Isaiah 42:16 NLT states, I will lead blind Israel down a new path, guiding them along an unfamiliar way. I will brighten the darkness before them and smooth out the road ahead of them. Yes, I will indeed do these things; I will not forsake them.* Allow Jesus to go before you removing the obstacles in your pathway and smoothing out the road ahead of you; this will help you to take those first important steps into an unfamiliar territory that God has prepared for you so you can depart from the land of Lo-debar. When Jesus is given the reigns to reign as Lord in your life—He is able to navigate us through the tempestuous storms of life.

Multiple Storms

A very dear friend and brother whom I will call William shared with me a series of tragic events that plunged him deep into Lo-debar, the dry place of no pasture. William and I have been friends for many years and I know him to be a true Man of God. When I met him many years ago he was married to a bright gifted woman with one child—over the years his family grew to include six more children.

The Lord blessed them with a thriving ministry built on prayer and conse-cration. They ministered a great deal on helping people get delivered from sexual perversion. At every level of promotion there will be a commensurate level of testing and their test came when one of their sons was molested by a family member. It was a very challenging situation for them that caused his wife to start questioning God. The molestation of her son was very difficult to deal with but was made worse by the fact that she was also molested at a very young age. Eventually she withdrew from the things of God and her withdrawal opened the door for the next tragic event. She became sexually in-volved with a man who was a business partner—a man who had broken bread in their house and presented himself as a friend. Infidelity is a terrible thing to deal with in a marriage but the situation is more egregious when the person sleeping with your wife or husband is someone you trusted—David declared, *"Yea, mine own familiar friend, in whom I trusted, which did eat of my bread, hath lifted up his heel against me" Psalm 41:9.*

William explained to me that he felt emasculated and dirty, it was as if his manhood was taken. It was rough enough trying to deal with the issue with his son then to be hit with the adulterous betrayal was more than he could handle. Because his wife refused to end the adulterous affair, he asked her to leave the home and her departure left him as the primary care giver for their seven children. The children were young and they had to deal with the repercussions of the separation. They could not understand why their mother had abandoned them. He found himself battling multiple storms simultaneously—the moles-tation, the adulterous affair, helping the children to deal with their mother not being in the home and the inability to get closure from the affair because the man sleeping with his wife used to pull his truck up in the driveway when she came to see the children.

He was driven deeper into Lo-debar, deeper into a dark place of depression and despair when she told him that God had brought that man into her life; he was the best thing that ever happened to her and gave her the best sex she ever had! Her words cut him deeply because many of the females around him when he was growing up told him that men were dogs and they did not take care of their family.

16

He was not naïve concerning the challenges married couples face but he never imagined that his marriage would reach a point where divorce was the only viable option.

Lord I don't want a Divorce!

In spite of the betrayal he tried very hard to keep the marriage from ending in divorce. Like Hosea with Gomer, he was willing to take her back and have the marriage restored through counseling. He realized that was not going to happen because she wanted to keep the man while maintaining some semblance of relationship with him—that was an unacceptable arrangement which made him realize the level of demonic infestation in her mind was too great and restoration and reconciliation were not possible.

William could not find the strength to pick up the Bible and could not pray. He was so weakened and debilitated by the tragic events that the things which could help him, prayer and the word, he could not engage in because of the depths of the sorrow in his soul. Many of the saints with whom he had fellowship when the anointing was flowing broke fellowship because some blamed him and some did not want to associate with him because of the breakup of the marriage. It was a very low time and season for him. In those times and seasons a person can feel forsaken by all and feel like the presence of the Lord is not with them. In such times it is important to remember the words of David, *"If I ascend up into heaven, thou art there: if I make my bed in hell, behold, thou art there" Psalm 139:8-11*. William felt alone in the deep dark place of Lo-debar but he would eventually find out that King Jesus is the friend that sticketh closer than a brother.

He contemplated suicide and he also contemplated the combination of murder suicide but thought about his precious children and the hurt it would cause them. One of the reasons he had difficulty picking up the Bible was a feeling he had of being unclean. Although he was not the one who defiled the marriage bed he still felt dirty.

When he thought things could not get worse he was hit with a financial storm because his wife's departure took a large part of the income that was brought into the house—on top of all the emotional trauma he was dealing with, he had to figure out how he would keep a roof over his children's head, as the bank threatened to foreclose on their home. In the Low place he had to battle feelings of low self-esteem, loneliness and feelings of being less than a man.

Defeating the Giants

William said he found himself facing some of the GIANTS of perversion he helped people to get deliverance from. Tragic situations can lead some people to binge eat, some to drink, and some to use and abuse drugs while others use illicit sex in an attempt to anesthetize themselves against the pain. When the marriage bed was defiled and he found himself sleeping alone and challenged to continue a life of consecration in the midst of feeling a need to satisfy his desire, not only for emotional companionship but a sexual one. There are individuals who turn to pornography, prostitution or some other illicit activity to numb or to deaden the pain of hurt and rejection. These sexually charged activities can and will open doors of addiction that can keep an individual bound for years.

William battled to maintain a posture of purity during that low period in his life. The maintenance of purity was very important to him because as a young adult he oversaw houses of ill repute. He made up his mind that he would not regress back to a time when his sex life was full of lust and perversion. This was challenging and difficult because the pain and rejection had caused him to pull away from things that he drew strength from which was prayer and reading the Bible.

A Mother in Zion

He did not have a great support system because he and his wife relocated to another state and had no family members there. When all appeared to be lost a mother in the church he attended at the time invited him to a divorce care class—at first he was very hesitant about going but she pressed him and he agreed.

In the class he met other individuals who were dealing with similar situations although not as deep. Ironically the turning point came for him one morning while he was in the shower. As he washed himself the Lord began to tell him that he was washing him and cleaning away the feelings that had him trapped in a low deplorable place—at that point he decided to take his mind's eye off his estranged wife, off the wolf who had crept into his home wearing sheep's clothing and off the other contrary things that were beating against his boat like a violent category five hurricane. He decided to look up and focus on his Savior Jesus. He came to the conclusion that he had to replace the negative feelings he had for her with forgiveness and prayer. Once his eyes were fixed on King Jesus and he began to pray for her—he could feel his heart and mind being lifted out of Lo-debar. Williams's transformation and deliverance from Lo-debar reminds me of a passage found in the Bible about Job. *"And the Lord turned the captivity of Job, when he prayed for his friends: also the Lord gave Job twice as much as he had before" Job 42:10.*

God is no respecter of persons and in the manner in which he delivered Job and William, he can do the same for you. There is no place or state so low and dark the light of God cannot shine there; just make up your mind that today is the last day you will spend in Lo-debar. Seek the Lord Jesus in prayer and through the word and He will restore you as He has restored countless others. Your change has come so it is time to make a change. The moving truck is here so pack up your thoughts and come out of Lo-debar.

Chapter 4

Who Dropped You? Part II

Who dropped you? Was it someone you trusted or someone to whom you were entrusted? Did they molest or rape you? Did they rob you of your innocence, causing you to have trust issues? It left you feeling abused and violated. Now you find yourself battling spirits of fear, rejection and low self-esteem. These spirits have caused you to retreat into a dark, desolate and lowly place where you find it difficult to have inner peace. Are you a male who was molested or raped by another male? Was that male a family member or a friend of the family? Are you wrestling with feelings of homosexuality—dealing with a gender identity crisis?

Are you a female who was dropped through molestation by another female and are you wrestling with same sex desires? It is extremely difficult to function effectively in a state of dysfunction. Some have entered into holy matrimony without being set free from the mental chains that have held them bound to a past of hurt and pain. Now they find it extremely difficult to give themselves wholeheartedly to their spouse. The marriage bed is supposed to be a place of unity and intimacy but there is an intruder there. The intruder is the nagging memory of being abused or being cheated on. The trust issues have caused you to become cold and rigid and now your spouse is thinking separation and divorce out of frustration. The marriage is fragmented and discombobulated because there is a great deal of hurt and pain from past experiences that are unresolved. The adverse effects of rape and molestation can have lifelong ramifications if not dealt with.

RIF: Rape, Incest, and Fratricide

King David had a beautiful daughter named Tamar and she was dropped because of rape by her brother Amnon, causing her to be so depressed that she put ashes on her head and hid herself in her brother Absalom's house. The family dysfunction did not begin with Amnon—it started with David. He slept with Bathsheba the wife of Uriah the Hittite then had his military commander send Uriah to the front of the battlefield so he could be killed. It is amazing the lengths people will go to satisfy and fulfill lustful desires. James declared, *"But every man is tempted, when he is drawn away of his own lust, and enticed. Then when lust hath conceived, it bringeth forth sin: and sin, when it is finished, bringeth forth death" James 1:14-15.* Mercy and Grace stays the executioner's hands when we are in sin, giving us an opportunity to repent by turning away from the sin back to God. Once we persist in the sinful behavior the end result will be death.

Judgment fell upon David's family when Amnon began to look at Tamar in a lustful perverted way. *"And it came to pass after this, that Absalom the son of David had a fair sister, whose name was Tamar; and Amnon the son of David loved her" 2 Samuel 13:1.* The love he had for her was not a brotherly love but an erotic love that a man has for a woman who is not related to him. *"And Amnon was so vexed, that he fell sick for his sister Tamar; for she was a virgin; and Amnon thought it hard for him to do anything to her" 2 Samuel 13:2.* He was consumed with a perverted desire for her to the point where he became sick. The Hebrew word for vexed as it is used there is the word yatsar—and it means to press, be narrow; be in distress: be straitened. His thoughts became so narrowly focused on her that it appears he could not keep his mind on anything else. He did not have easy access to her because she stayed in an apartment where the king's unmarried daughters resided. His lust-laden and perverted desire fueled his ungodly persistence. Instead of seeking counseling—He allowed his friend and cousin Jonadab who the Bible describes as being subtil—to concoct a diabolical plan to lure the unsuspecting Tamar into his web of deceit. The Hebrew word for subtil as it is used there is the word chakam and it means wise, skilful or cunning. He told Amnon to feign sickness and when David came to see him to request that he send Tamar to fix him some meat. David swallowed the bait—hook, line and sinker.

Once she finished cooking he lured her into the chamber, took hold of her and asked her to sleep with him. And she answered him, Nay, my brother, do not force me; for no such thing ought to be done in Israel: do not thou this folly And I, whither shall I cause my shame to go? And as for thee, thou shalt be as one of the fools in Israel. *Now therefore, I pray thee, speak unto the king; for he will not withhold me from thee, 2 Samuel 13:12-13.* She probably told him to speak to the king because she was desperate to free herself from his lust-laden tentacles.

Howbeit he would not hearken unto her voice: but, being stronger than she, forced her, and lay with her, 2 Samuel 13:14. Once his cousin and friend Jonadab put the idea in his head, he lost all sense of reason where she was concerned. Lust and perversion can consume a mind to the point where a person is willing to risk everything jeopardizing their life and forsaking their position, their reputation, their wife, their children, and their security and even their freedom to fulfill one brief, reckless moment of unrestrained sinful pleasure. After he finished with her he hated her exceedingly—at that point his hatred for her exceeded the love he claimed to have had for her so he asked her to leave. She pleaded with him not to put her out but he called his servant and told him, *"Put now this woman out from me, and bolt the door after her"*
2 Samuel 13:17.

Before, she was Tamar whom he loved but now that he has defiled and shamed her, she is just a woman who deserved to be put out; abandoned and discarded. Previously he saw her through the lens of lust but now when he looked at her she became merely an object who reminded him of his degrading act and he saw her with the eyes of contempt and disdain. He would not even call her by her name, instead she became, "this woman." The fact that he told his servant to bolt the door meant he never wanted to see her again. He took her virginity and in that culture it meant shame and disgrace because he was not her husband. The matter was worsened by the fact he was her brother so she had to deal with a double shame; losing her virginity by rape and being the victim of incest. There are many men and women like Tamar, who are carrying the guilt and shame of rape and molestation, some of them by a family member or someone thought to be a family friend. The rape and molestation have left them feeling marred, scarred and emotionally incapacitated.

The Bible describes Tamar as having a garment of divers colors upon her: for with such robes were the king's daughters that were virgins apparelled. The degrading feelings and the residual effects of rape and molestation cannot be covered by royal apparel—especially when the violation came at the claws of a friend or family member. Tamar's brother was supposed to be her protector but uncontrolled, ungodly desires caused him to be her violator. *Then his servant brought her out, and bolted the door after her. And Tamar put ashes on her head, and rent her garment of divers colors that was on her, and laid her hand on her head, and went on crying, 2 Samuel 13:18-19.* Renting her garment, putting ashes on her head and placing her hand on her head were signs of shame and disgrace. There are individuals in our midst who don't have the look of being violated because they go to great lengths to maintain a veneer and a facade that mask the deep seated hurt and pain they endure.

To the men and women who continue to suffer from the shame of being violated, I encourage you from the word of God by letting you know—you do not have to live in a dark desolate place of mental and emotional anguish because God will give you beauty for ashes and the garment of praise for the spirit of heaviness. He will give you the oil of joy for mourning. The loss of her virginity to her brother and the ensuing shame that it caused was like a death to her. Thanks be to God for King Jesus—the restorer of the brokenhearted, the repairer of the breach, His precious blood cleanses those who have been defiled because His blood cleanses us from all sin. *Therefore if any man be in Christ, he is a new creature: old things are passed away; behold, all things are become new 2 Corinthians 5:17.* The Greek word for creature as it is used by Paul is the word ktisis; it means a building, an ordinance or creation. In his first letter to the church at Corinth he told them they were God's husbandry, God's building. In order to understand the significance of this we have to look at the epistle of Peter which states, *"But ye are a chosen generation, a royal priesthood, an holy nation, a peculiar people; that ye should shew forth the praises of him who hath called you out of darkness into his marvellous light" 1 Peter 2:9.* Prior to coming to the saving knowledge of the Lord Jesus Christ, all of us were dwelling in a low dark place; by grace through faith we were washed in the blood and became reconstructed temples from which His glorious light can shine.

If you are living a life outside of Jesus the Ark of safety, it is important for you to know; there is no shame so deep; no sin so grievous, no wound so injurious that He is not able to bring healing and restoration. Please allow Him to cleanse you of all feelings of shame and disgrace and allow Him to purify you with the transforming power of His Spirit.

Vengeance is Mine Saith the Lord!

When Amnon told his cousin Jonadab how he loved Tamar, he described her in this manner; *"I love Tamar, my brother Absalom's sister" 2 Samuel 13:4*. In many countries where polygamy prevails, the girls are considered to be under the special care and protection of their uterine brother. A uterine brother is one who shares the same mother but not the same father. The uterine brother is the guardian of their interests and their honor, even more than their father himself. Absalom was that brother and guardian. He waited two years to exact revenge on Amnon and then he had his servants kill him. The Bible describes Tamar as remaining desolate in her brother Absalom's house. Rape, Incest and Fratricide—WOW!!! And some of us think our families are dysfunctional.

Tamar was not complicit in any way shape or form in the act perpetrated upon her. She was an innocent victim of rape and incest. She simply desired to help her brother. There are many instances where a woman is raped then further victimized by narrow-minded people who suggest she did something to abet and encourage it. It is a way of blaming the victim and no victim should have to endure additional trauma while trying to deal with what they have gone through. There are many events that may have transpired years ago in one's life that has caused hurt and pain. If this pain is not dealt with and continues to linger indefinitely, the end result could be harmful to one's present and cause unnecessary delay of a fruitful future. When you come to Christ, you are a new creation, cleansed by His blood and accompanied by His word and the Holy Spirit as your guide to lead you into a victorious life. In order to make progress in your life, you must first stop reliving the traumas of your past that have left you scarred. Go to Jesus who is the great Physician and Healer. Lastly, allow Him to heal your scarred tissues. Let Him operate!

Who Dropped You? Was it a former pastor, church leader or a lay member? Instead of covering your frailty they chose to expose and excommunicate you. As a young Christian I heard people say how terrible it was to suffer church hurt. After experiencing it I realized firsthand what they meant. Church is supposed to be the place where the body of Christ gather together in unity and on one accord, not for religious activities but to praise and worship God—to receive a word from Him and to have fellowship one with another. Unfortunately the church can be the place where a person may have to deal with backbiting gossip, judgments, betrayal or even false accusation—not to mention nepotism, cronyism, cliques and jealousy. There are individuals who have been so wounded in the church they refuse to go back and some have turned back from the faith because the pain is unbearable.

Who Dropped You? Was it a parent who favored another sibling over you? No matter what you did to gain their approval it was never enough in their eyes. Your sibling was excused for the greatest of transgressions while you were vilified for the slightest infraction. Your hope and expectation was to be a part of a loving family—a family where you would be nurtured and encouraged to become someone great. Instead of feeling love and affection you felt hurt and pain because of the favoritism and it left you feeling unappreciated and undervalued. You are all grown up now with your own family but you have not been able to be freed from the memories of your early childhood and how desperately you tried to please your mother or father or both but it was all in vain inciting sibling rivalry that continues to this day.

Joseph was dropped by his brothers because he was his father's favorite and that favoritism was symbolized by the coat of many colors that he received. They threw him into a dry pit; he was sold into slavery, falsely accused of rape and forgotten about in prison. His dream of how he would be used by God is the trigger that enraged them but the underlying root of the bitterness was the jealousy they had in their hearts because of the way their father gave him preferential treatment which they greatly resented. When Joseph was languishing in prison, thinking the butler had forgotten about him, that was when he was promoted to his regal position in the court of Pharaoh—God was preparing to give Pharaoh a dream that would set in motion the release of Joseph from prison and his subsequent promotion.

You may be in an uncomfortable place or situation at the present time, you may feel like others have forgotten you but I want you to know that God has not forgotten you and He has a plan for your life.

God in His infinite mercy and grace will remember you; He is attentive towards you; He keeps a constant vigil over you. God is always aware of your existence whether you acknowledge God's existence or not. God thinks so much of you and is so concerned for you as His child that His hand bears the inscription of your name held ever before Him. *"Behold, I have engraved you on the palms of my hands; your walls are continually before me." Isaiah 49:16 ESV.* God keeps you on His mind and His thoughts are continually toward you; this relentless wakeful consciousness is expressed *in Psalm 8:4; "What is man, that thou art mindful of him? and the son of man, that thou visitest him." Also in Psalm 121:4 "God neither slumbers nor sleeps."* He is aware of your being even in times when He seems the most distant and remote and yet God's ever-looming presence is there, *"Am I a God at hand, saith the Lord,"* and not a God afar off? *Can any hide himself in secret places that I shall not see him? saith the Lord. Do not I fill heaven and earth? saith the Lord Jeremiah 23:23-24.*

Do not despair beloved or be weary in well-doing but continue to hold fast to your profession of faith despite what you are experiencing. *Hebrews 10:23* says, *"Let us hold fast the profession of our faith without wavering; for he is faithful that promised."* Hold tightly to your dreams, your visions, your promises, and your word from God. Never give up hope in God fulfilling them and bringing them to pass because your Heavenly Father is knowledgeable and attentive to your plight and refuses to leave you suffering in a place of darkness, in a dry and thirsty place without any pasture in the land of Lo-debar. Because of God's covenant, Lo-debar is not a permanent dwelling place for His children and neither was it for Mephibosheth. God will catapult you out of the depths of your low place for His plan, His purpose, His glory and will place you in a high place; *"He maketh my feet like hinds' feet, and setteth me upon my high places." Psalm 18:33.*

God raises the poor out of the dust, He lifts up the needy out of the dunghill, He picks us up out of the gutter, He elevates us out of the pig-pen, He digs us out of the miry pit, He cuts the iron shackles of our self-imposed prison, he propels us out of the land of Lo-debar, a place of lameness, incapacitation, immobility and shame into the land of the living. God transports us to a land of plenty, a land of lush, fertile pastures and green rolling hills, a land of fruitfulness and flourishing vegetation, a land of richness and fatness.

At the appointed time, at the assigned year, at the designated season, at the ordained month and day, at the chosen hour, at the lifting of God's sovereign right hand, at the divine directive and commission, at the execution of the utmost, final commanding order and providence of our great and mighty, God He has set a time to fulfill every purpose in heaven to occur on this earth. God orchestrates and directs our steps. God oversees every scintilla of our lives so if God has envisioned it, if God has written it, if God has willed it, if God has promised it, if God has sworn it, if anything has proceeded out of the mouth of God; God will perform it, God will accomplish it, God will honor it, it shall come to pass; it must be done! It does not matter what it looks like now, it does not matter how long it takes, it does not matter how inconceivable, no matter how farfetched and unattainable it may seem in the natural, one day all the myriad of things you have been dreaming and hoping for will ultimately be realized. *Habakkuk 2:3* declares, *"For the vision is yet for an appointed time, but at the end it shall speak, and not lie: though it tarry, wait for it; because it will surely come, it will not tarry."* We cannot facilitate it neither can we force anything to happen before its time.

Mephibosheth went from being a titled royal prince with vast wealth and prosperity to becoming a disheveled, unkempt penniless pauper and peasant with no house or property of his own; relegated to the low status of a commoner. After several years had passed and he became an adult (references in the Dake's Bible refer to his age between 17-23 when the king sought to bless someone from the house of Saul for Jonathan's sake)—King David thought to show him kindness and consideration but it took some time. It may seem that God is taking His time but always remember God never forgets His covenant with His children; He never drops us, He never forsakes us, He never abandons us.

God does not forget us because He is our Father; He created us to be His children. Note the words in the following scripture: *Isaiah 49:15 ESV, "Can a woman forget her nursing child, that she should have no compassion on the son of her womb? Even these may forget, yet I will not forget you."* When others drop us, God is faithful. God will be waiting with open arms to keep us and shelter us but only if we give Him the opportunity. *"He will wipe away all tears from our eyes." Revelation 21:4.* He will smooth our troubled brow; He is the lifter of our weary head, He will prove His fatherly love for us time and time again and gently and compassionately pick us up when we fall. *"The eternal God is thy refuge, and underneath are the everlasting arms." Deuteronomy 33:27.*

Do not allow your present circumstance or situation to deflate or depress you. Do not allow anyone to define you by what you are going through at the present time because greater is up ahead. Your position and your condition do not negate the plan of God for your life. He will use your present position and condition for His glory if you are willing to surrender. Association brings assimilation so don't resign yourself mentally or physically to the low place.

Don't Identify Me by the Infirmity

Good intentions don't always produce good results. When David was bringing the ark back to Jerusalem he put it on a cart. At some point in the journey the cart hit a bump in the road and Uzzah touched it fearing it would fall—he lost his life because the anger of the Lord was kindled against him. He was not supposed to touch the ark. He died instantly right by the presence of God. You are called to live in His presence, not to die by His presence. What you consider to be a good thing is not always sanctioned and approved by God and that is why it is necessary to ascertain the will of God through His word or by seeking direction from the Holy Spirit.

Mephibosheth's nurse thought she was doing a good thing when she fearfully picked him up and fled hastily. She thought she was on her way to a place of safety but she caused him to hit a bump in the road in the journey of his life that would now be marked with tragedy.

That one unforeseeable bump in the road diverted him to Lo-debar rearranging the plans for his life. His nurse's good deed of trying to preserve his life would change the course and direction of his life through no fault of his own.

After reading about him becoming lame in his feet—the next time we hear about him is when King David remembered the covenant with Mephibosheth's father Jonathan. He began looking for anyone who was left of the house of Saul so he could show them kindness for Jonathan's sake. As previously stated, David had made a covenant with Jonathan Saul's son to be a blessing. Covenants were taken very seriously in that culture because they represented a binding agreement. God made a covenant with Abraham to show kindness unto the Gentiles for his sake. When God made the covenant with him He had none greater to swear by so he swore by Himself. Through the covenant He would bless all the families of the earth. Once a covenant was made the parties involved were sworn to it so David was very diligent in his search for an heir of Jonathan so he could fulfill his covenant promise to Jonathan.

David was informed by one of the servants of the house of Saul by the name of Ziba, that Jonathan had a son who was lame of his feet. Funny how some people choose to identify us by some affliction or lameness, by some physical imperfection or emotional flaw we are dealing with or have dealt with? David asked if anyone was left of the house of Saul, not about their condition. I am reminded of the time when Jesus asked the man at the pool of Bethesda if he would like to be made whole—the man decided to give Jesus the history of the lack of help he received from others when the angels troubled the water. Bethesda means house of mercy, a reservoir. It consisted of five porches and five is symbolic of grace. Beloved, when merciful King Jesus comes to shower you with grace and a reservoir of blessings, please do not talk about the past and the people who did not help you, please do not rationalize or make excuses, please do not garner pity for yourself—just say, Yes Lord!

Your lameness should not define who you are or be a stumbling block to you becoming the person God created you to be. Whatever the lameness, it should be a stepping stone to greatness and not a hindrance.

People who have a discerning eye should be able to see beyond any liability and know there is great ability. Shallow-minded individuals who lack vision and insight will only see lameness but someone with the eyes of an eagle will see your greatness from a mile away. Chickens only see what is on the ground or directly in front of them but eagles are visionaries, they have insight and foresight. True visionaries can see beyond the rough where there is a diamond waiting to be cut and polished. How many times have people overlooked a treasure because they focused their attention on the exterior and were unable to see the greatness beyond the surface? There are people who have gone to yard sales and flea markets and something that was overlooked and passed over by others they sensed its inherent worth and value and walked out with something they paid very little for only to find out later it was very valuable.

PART 2:

HELP I'VE FALLEN AND I CAN'T GET UP

Chapter 5

Sabrina's Story

Have you ever seen certain signs but chose not to follow them? Warning signs that told you not to proceed but you ignored them because your desire for something obscured the reality that should have been evident. The further you travelled the more you realized you were on the wrong road but felt you could not exit or make a U-turn. Eventually at the end of the road you were forced to make a U-turn. I'm going to tell you about my story and the U-turn I was forced to make when I ignored the signs and my life spiraled out of control. My story is called Sabrina's story and it is a story of triumph over tragedy!

In the Beginning

I was raised in the Christian home of a pastor/bishop. The fact that I was the eldest child and the pastor and first lady's daughter meant my life was lived under a microscope. I had to walk a fine line because it seemed some people were waiting for the pastor's daughter to mess up. Only a PK, a preacher's kid can fully understand the pressures associated with being the son or daughter of the leader. After graduating high school I decided to go away to college. I desired a good education but I felt I needed to get out of my parent's house in order to establish my own identity. While living in Euclid, Ohio I was introduced to a man via the phone by my mom. In conversations with him I thought to myself, he's the one, but something deep down inside told me to be cautious.

As the conversation between me and Tyrone developed, I decided to fly home to meet him. At first I thought to myself, this is a joke, never met him face to face but only spoke with him over the phone and now I'm coming home for a short visit to meet a man my mother feels is my husband. Despite the reservations that I had, I thought to myself, if my mom loves him I should too. I was young and pretty naïve back then.

After the tragedy of September 11 I decided to move back home because I missed my family and decided to marry Tyrone. He appeared to be the ideal man of color; dark, sexy, thick two hundred plus pounds, body building physique, a fine all milky chocolate man. He was an ex-stripper then he got saved right after he was discharged from the army. He joined my father's church and became his armor bearer; he was very gifted and presented himself as a dedicated servant of the Lord. He projected an image and public persona that made him look like an attractive candidate for wedlock. Tyrone told me he loved me that he would take care of me and he wanted to have children right way, so I said I do; Till this very day in my heart I felt that my marriage was arranged. Before I got married I noticed there were many things wrong with him. He was prone to sudden outbursts, crying and would cuss me out over simple things. I wanted to stay on this journey of getting married, because all of my girlfriends were now married and I felt left out.

I would have these conversations with myself about yes marry him, no don't marry him and maybe so. On June 1st I closed my eyes and got married. The wedding was everything I dreamed of—five hundred plus guests, sixty two people in the bridal party. Everyone was dressed in black and white. I gave out long stemmed roses as I came down the aisle. There was a horse and carriage, it was a true Cinderella Story; finally a dream come true, my heart's desire fulfilled—then ninety days being newly married I found out I was pregnant. The pregnancy represented the fulfillment of another dream; the dream of having a family. It did not take long for the dream to turn into a nightmare. During my pregnancy the verbal abuse escalated and the sexual abuse started. He would come home after working out in the sun all day without taking a shower, hold me down and force himself in me—can a married man rape his wife?

Not only was I living a lie, but here is the bishop's daughter living with an abusive husband who was verbally, mentally, physically, emotionally and sexually abusive. I was under so much stress that whatever was going on in my personal life would eventually cause me to have a miscarriage.

During our courtship we went to marriage counseling to a renowned doctor who knew me from my youth, and I found out after my divorce that my ex-husband disclosed some information to this particular pastor/Dr. pertaining to some sexual demons that laid dormant in his life. I questioned God concerning the reason the doctor did not disclose that information to me. Did she purposely want me to fail by getting married to a man she knew had issues? Why, why didn't she inform me that this marriage would probably end up in a divorce and was on an endless road to HELL?

It was November 21 when I woke up to use the bathroom when I realized I was bleeding. I tried to stop the flow but it kept coming out—then I felt a head with hair so I called 911 and was rushed to the hospital where I had to continue giving birth to my first child. Josiah was his name and I was five and a half months at the time. I thank God my girlfriend was there because I didn't want to see the baby. She helped me push out the afterbirth; this was a hard time for me. Satan was playing tricks on my mind making me feel like I was not good enough to be a mother.

Tyrone played the role of comforting me; he played it so well making me feel like I was the only woman in his sight. Although I felt he was responsible for the miscarriage because of the stress and duress he had me under. I found out ninety days later that I was pregnant again. My body didn't have time to heal before getting pregnant and the abuse started all over. I started seeing an ob-gyn specialist who deemed me high risk due to me losing my first son and now pregnant 90 days after that loss. Again we were instructed not to engage in any form of sexual activity. One particular day Tyrone came home smelling like a different woman and strange soap. When you're pregnant your senses are very sharp. I knew the smell meant he had been with another woman but I still embraced my role as the ideal wife.

I made sure he had a cooked meal ready for him when he came home from work. I engaged him in conversation, inquiring how his day went. No matter how ideal a wife I felt I was it was never enough for Tyrone—his response to me was based on the type of mood he was in. When I asked him of the smell of another woman that was on him he tossed his dinner across the room because he was so angry that I could smell the scent of someone else on him—as far as he was concerned, I was out of line as his wife to question him. He was the quintessential male chauvinist.

My Physical Abuse

I remember one day he got so angry with me that he tried to press a hot iron against my face while he told me "I love you and you can never leave me." Some people have a twisted way of expressing what they call love. I ran into the closet holding the bottom of my belly praying "Lord do not let me lose this child; I was still battling depression from losing Josiah and losing this child would drive me into a deeper place of despair. I held on to the door screaming help me! Help me!

Like a falling leaf from a tree, three of my fingers were dangling from my hand because he tried to yank open the closet door while I was holding on for dear life. I had to scream out his name. Tyrone! Stop I'm bleeding! I'm bleeding—he looked at me with hate and disdain, then looked at my fingers and said, 'bitch' "go get it fixed."

I called my girlfriend who followed me to the hospital and I begged her not to tell the truth about what happened. They asked me repeatedly are you in an abusive marriage, are you afraid to go back home and I said no; yet in my mind I'm thinking how could the bishop's daughter let the world know that she's in an abusive marriage and in fear of her life? What would the church folks think about the bishop's daughter, youth and choir director if they knew she was living in a marriage that had a pleasant veneer in public but was HELL in private?

Time is Passing

I'm happy that finally five and a half months passed and I thought yes lord! I will not lose this baby then it's the sixth month and I start experiencing excruciating pain. My water broke again and I was rushed to the hospital. When I arrived at the hospital I gave birth to Jeremiah, who died shortly thereafter—I looked at him, I combed his hair, I counted his fingers, toes and noticed that his eyes were still fused. I realized God was not finished making him. Life can seem so cruel at times; all I ever wanted was a happy marriage with children. Hate began to set in, accompanied by anger and rage. I was not only angry with Tyrone for abusing me and causing me to experience such great loss; I was angry with God this time—I was angry with Him because I felt He knew that I was going to lose my baby and all I kept saying was why me again?

Two mothers in the church came to my house to pray with me. I confided in them the things Tyrone was doing to me and they told me I could not leave him. I felt confused because they counseled me on the subject of FORGIVENESS but did not seem to understand the mental torment I was enduring. They told me, God would not put more on me than I could bear. Church was all I knew and we were never taught about transparency. It was all about maintaining a certain public image.

Slowly Healing

In your darkest loneliest place where you can feel abandoned and forsaken, God will have someone there to encourage you; someone who can see the low place you are in and take the time to comfort you. I will be forever thankful for my friend. Her unconditional love, support, listening ear and wisdom helped me to hope again. A few months after my loss, I made the decision not to live out the rest of my life as a bitter, angry woman. I realized I had too much life ahead of me and I was going to live out the plans that God had for my life and not let the enemy rob me from that. So, I chose to forgive Tyrone and once again I was pregnant. The tragedy of losing two children did not take away my desire to have a family but in the back of my mind I had mixed emotions. On the one hand I felt joy in knowing that I was going to have a baby but I was nervous because of the previous losses.

It's a normal day for my doctor's appointment, a routine checkup to find out if everything is fine with this third pregnancy. After a culture test was done I found out I had something called Chlamydia. I sat in a chair and cried for hours asking God, how do I stay with a man who can't keep his penis to himself? I was instructed that Tyrone and I needed medication and once again was told NO MORE sexual activity. NO GOD, not another baby lost. I should've walked away from him; the STD should've been the final straw but I was taught that a wife had to stick with her husband. The word on forgiveness given to me by the two mothers kept ringing in my ears.

Now let me just say that forgiveness is a process but you have to make the decision that you are going to forgive in order to move forward. Here I am trying to move on in my heart with losing Josiah and Jeremiah, and now I have to deal with the prospect of losing my third baby.

The day finally came when I lost my last son whom I named Zachary Jaden after giving birth. I tried talking to God but found out that it was a process I was going through. Before my loss I was informed that Tyrone cheated on me with someone in my church who happened to be an old friend. *"For it was not an enemy that reproached me; then I could have borne it: neither was it he that hated me that did magnify himself against me; then I would have hid myself from him: But it was thou, a man mine equal, my guide, and mine acquaintance. We took sweet counsel together and walked unto the house of God in company" Psalm 55:12-14*. The depth of the level of that betrayal left me unwilling to trust others. That particular friend was very close to me. She ate at my table and I confided many things in her. I never dreamed she would sleep with my husband.

A meeting was called with him and my old friend and the experience was very painful. It was so painful that I told him to leave the house as I tried to process everything. All I wanted was a peaceful pregnancy and a husband who loved me. Before I could think about taking him back I told him to tell me every woman that he was involved with and he wrote down the names of two women in my church and thirty different women outside. Living with an abusive man who cheated thirty-two times in the marriage, including multiple times with women you know, can leave you feeling empty and void of self-worth.

38

I made a decision to keep moving forward regardless of whether I stayed with my husband or not. I, my family, our friends and several people from the church chose to walk down that road; the road to file for a divorce which I thought would give me true deliverance. When the divorce papers were signed I should have breathed a sigh of relief but I blacked out. Legally I was out of the marriage but divorce papers do not instantly remove the residual feelings of depression and low self-esteem as you attempt to put the pieces back together. I found it very difficult to sleep and had to take sleeping pills. I sunk so low into depression and hopelessness that I despaired of life.

One day I found myself standing on a bridge ready to jump when a man who was fishing, walked up to me and said—"it's not worth it, God would not put more on you than you can bear and He will see you through this." I had called siblings to say goodbye and they came and found me on the bridge and encouraged me to keep living. When I asked them about the man who was fishing they said there was no man there; he was probably an angel sent by God to keep me from ending my life. I know it is probably difficult for someone who has never suffered a time of deep depression to understand—how a person could get to the place where she was willing to end her life. I hope you never have to experience despair that is so deep that death seems to be a more suitable option than living. Eventually I remarried and gave birth to a beautiful daughter; my turnaround didn't come overnight, it was a process and it took time to get to a place of relief especially from being tormented by negative memories of a failed marriage to Tyrone and his trysts with the other women, but today thank God I am Free.!!!

Chapter 6

·

Lo-debar

After informing David that Jonathan had a son who was lame on his feet, David asked Ziba where he was. He told him Mephibosheth was in the house of Machir, the son of Ammiel, in Lo-debar. One mishap in life can cause many years of pain and suffering. One bad decision can have lifelong consequences. Mephibosheth's grandfather Saul started out with a lot of promise when he was anointed to be king but his lack of fortitude in obeying God caused his kingdom to topple and be taken from him and given to another. His disobedience had a ripple effect because his son Jonathan wound up dying on the battlefield with him. Jonathan had a lot of class and character but sometimes the family we are born into has a direct impact on what we will become later in life.

The terrifying news of Saul's and Jonathon's death caused the nurse to make a hasty move that resulted in the crippling of the feet of Mephibosheth. On a cautionary note, we have to be extremely careful not to act impulsively making decisions without consulting God and without much forethought or reasoning because of the potentially harmful repercussions of those decisions affecting our loved ones and others, not just in our lives but in generations to come. The greatest example of this is when Adam decided to rebel against God by taking part in what Eve had done. His actions opened the door for sin and death to plague the entire human race. When Abram decided to sleep with Sarai's maid, he did not realize the magnitude of the problem the birth of Ishmael would cost. Look at the bloodshed and carnage in the Middle East today and you will see what one man's decision to birth an Ishmael in the waiting room does.

My Lo-debar the Pig Pen

When I made the decision to smuggle drugs to England years ago, I was not thinking about the possibility that I might get caught and what it would mean for my wife and young children. All I could see was the dollar signs. It was only after I was caught and put on remand in a cell without a toilet and given an eight year sentence that I began to reflect on the fact that my actions had exposed my wife and children to suffering and poverty. When I was sent to the Isle of Sheppey, an island off the northern coast of Kent in England to serve my sentence—it did not take me long to find out that the prison was built near a pig's farm. When the wind blew the stench of the pigs invaded my cell. North in the scriptures is indicative of judgment and disaster. I was judged for my crime and it was a disaster for me and my family—BUT GOD!!! It was a low place but the King; the good Shepherd transformed my life through the Word of God and through the Spirit of God. I thank Him for taking me out of the low place of no pasture; I thank Him for giving me life and that more abundantly.

No Pasture—No Pastor

Instead of living in his own house like a prince and the grandson of a king—he is lame in Lo-debar, a prince living like a pauper. As previously stated Lo-debar means no pasture, no pasture meant he was living in a low infertile place. One of the Hebrew words for pasture is—mir`eh pronounced meer-eh' and it means, a feeding place. It comes from the root word ra`ah pronounced raw-aw'; and it means to tend a flock, to graze, to make friendship with or companionship, to pastor, or to shepherd. He was not only in an infertile place, but a place that lacked companionship and true friendship. Later when we hear his response to David when he came to bless him we will get greater insight into his mental state in Lo-debar. His situation was made more challenging by the fact that he was lame in his feet living in Lo-debar—that meant he was dependent on others because the people of that day and culture had to work long hours in the fields. Being lame in the feet is tough enough but to be that way, living in someone's house, in a dry and lonely place is terrible. There are several verses in the Bible that deal with the word pasture in terms of abundance or the lack thereof.

41

When God used Pharaoh to promote Joseph out of the prison of Lo-debar, He did it to put Joseph in position to preserve posterity for his father's house. Joseph's father and his brethren were dwelling in Canaan and there was a famine in that land. When they arrived in Egypt, *"They said moreover unto Pharaoh, For to sojourn in the land are we come; for thy servants have no pasture for their flocks; for the famine is sore in the land of Canaan: now therefore, we pray thee, let thy servants dwell in the land of Goshen" Genesis 47:4.* Goshen was situated on the east of the Nile, not far from the royal residence. East is a godly direction so it is not surprising that the direction where they were situated was eastward. It was the best of the land. You can be in a dry place, a place of no pasture but because of your connection to the God of the covenant, you can be confident that He will lead you to a good and fertile land. You may be experiencing famine-like conditions at the moment. You may be in a lackluster marriage where you are not receiving companionship, love and true friendship—you may feel like you have hit a brick wall and your life is stagnant but do not allow your mental faculty to succumb to the negativity of the situation. You are one encounter away from your deliverance.

David was the king used by God to bless and restore Mephibosheth—Jesus is the King sent by God to bless and restore you. Are you reading this book from Lo-debar, from a low place of despair and depression? Is your Lo-debar a physical, a mental place or both? Is your Lo-debar a small prison cell where you have been confined for many years battling forces that are trying to drive you into a deep place of degradation? Is it a medical situation that has you in a very bleak state of mind? Is it a mental state of utter despair and depression where you feel hopeless? Is it the effects of the separation or divorce that have left you feeling like your future is uncertain? I want to encourage you not to lose hope because the King desires an audience with you. God will not leave you in a dry place, a place of famine and lack. The story of Joseph and his family is a great example of overcoming tragic situations by trusting God. Joseph suffered betrayal but did not allow the gravity of his situation to plunge him into a place of despair. He trusted in God's providence and that trust allowed him to see the divine plan of God in the betrayal.

IT'S TIME TO COME OUT OF LO-DEBAR

Once he was able to see God's guiding hand in his situation, he was able to bless his brothers who betrayed him. He was able to be a blessing to them and his father's entire household when they came to Egypt.

"And Pharaoh spake unto Joseph, saying, Thy father and thy brethren are come unto thee: The land of Egypt is before thee; in the best of the land make thy father and brethren to dwell; in the land of Goshen let them dwell: and if thou knowest any men of activity among them, then make them rulers over my cattle. And Joseph brought in Jacob his father, and set him before Pharaoh: and Jacob blessed Pharaoh" Genesis 47:5-7. Pharaoh was blessed by the Patriarch Jacob. One moment Jacob was dealing with a famine in Canaan and the next moment he is blessing and being blessed by Pharaoh. That is the reason why we must have mental fortitude to survive the low place. Some people have given up right when they were on the cusp of their breakthrough. Jacob refused to allow the famine to destroy his family— *"now when Jacob saw that there was corn in Egypt, Jacob said unto his sons, Why do ye look one upon another? And he said, Behold, I have heard that there is corn in Egypt: get you down thither, and buy for us from thence; that we may live, and not die"* Genesis 42:1-2.

Jacob was admonishing his sons to get to Egypt to buy corn; he was oblivious of the fact that his son Joseph was strategically positioned there to preserve posterity for him and the rest of his household. Jacob thought Joseph was dead; When you are in Lo-debar people may think you are gone for good but in due season when it is time for you to fulfill your divine assignment, God will elevate you as He did with Joseph. Like Joseph, we must remember that the Lord is with us, in good times and in bad.

When you are in a low place mentally it will have a detrimental effect on you physically and spiritually. Spiritually these are the times when you feel as if God is far away; In those times you find no rest, refreshment or pasture. There are people who suffer from deep depression who keep their curtains drawn and stay in the bed; sometimes they feel so weakened by their condition that they cannot even get out of bed. Jacob told his sons to stop looking at each other and move in the direction where there was corn.

43

When you are in a low place, a place of no pasture, you do not need to look at people looking at you—you need someone in the midst with an ear to hear where the sustenance is; once we determine where it is you have to be willing to go. Fear will stagnate and cripple; like the four lepers whose story is told in, you must not allow your condition to debilitate and suffocate your life.

The four lepers sat by a gate in Samaria during a severe famine. As lepers they were supposed to be confined to a certain area but they refused to die in a place of no pasture. When they took the initiative to move they found a camp abandoned by the enemy that was loaded with food, drink, silver, gold and raiment. Mephibosheth's lame feet were a problem but his biggest problem was that he allowed his mental state to become lame with depression and low self-esteem. I challenge you to have the determination to rise above any circumstance or situation that seeks to keep you stuck in the low place—thought precedes action so if you can think it then you can achieve it.

Covenant Keeper

David could have put his feet up and enjoyed the fat of the land when he became king over all Israel and Judah but he remembered the promise he had made to Jonathan in the form of a covenant. Jonathan and David made a covenant because he loved him as his own soul. *"And Jonathan stripped himself of the robe that was upon him, and gave it to David, and his garments, even to his sword, and to his bow, and to his girdle" 1 Samuel 18:3-4.* Jonathan stripping himself of his robe and giving it to David had great significance.

Jonathan was being groomed to be Saul's successor but He recognized that David was God's choice and he was humble enough to submit himself. Saul's anger was kindled against Jonathan when he refused to turn against David. He told Jonathan that he would not be established, nor his kingdom as long as David lived. If a person does not have discernment then they better have caller ID. We have to be humble enough to flow with the person through whom God is working. David never forgot the kindness of Jonathan.

There are individuals who have promised to bless you and when they came into their blessing they stopped returning your phone calls and even changed their number. Mephibosheth's restoration depended on the covenant between his father and David. Mephibosheth was not born at the time the covenant was established between his father and David. Before he came into this world he had favor with the future King. The nurse dropping him and his lack of knowledge of the favor did not negate it. He just needed to be given the opportunity to take possession of it as did eventually happen.

The people who are lame in Lo-debar at the present time do not have knowledge of the King's covenant. The Lamb was slain from the foundation of the world and there are names written in the book of life from the foundation of the world. In the letter to the Church at Ephesus the Apostle Paul wrote about a people who have been predestinated. Here is what he had to say, *"Blessed be the God and Father of our Lord Jesus Christ, who hath blessed us with all spiritual blessings in heavenly places in Christ: According as he hath chosen us in him before the foundation of the world, that we should be holy and without blame before him in love: Having predestinated us unto the adoption of children by Jesus Christ to himself, according to the good pleasure of his will"* Ephesians 1:3-5.

Personally I do not believe those verses are saying some people were born to damnation and never had a hope of being saved, while others were predestined to be saved—I believe in God's Omniscience, there is the foreknowledge of the people who would accept Jesus and those who would not. We have to witness because we do not have that omniscience and foreknowledge. Before Mephibosheth was born, his father and David knew there was a covenant which contained blessings for Jonathan's seed. David was willing to leave the comfort of the palace to find anyone of the house of Saul so he could show him kindness. When David was under attack from Saul, Jonathan knew that the Lord would protect him and this is what he said to David, *"And thou shalt not only while yet I live shew me the kindness of the Lord, that I die not: But also thou shalt not cut off thy kindness from my house for ever: no, not when the Lord hath cut off the enemies of David every one from the face of the earth.*

Lo-debar

So Jonathan made a covenant with the house of David, saying, Let the Lord even require it at the hand of David's enemies" 1 Samuel 20:14-16. Jonathan was a prince and mighty warrior when David was running for his life but he was able to discern the calling of God that was on David. People who lack true discernment will not be able to see you beyond the place of your current struggle and because of the lack of true discernment they will identify you based your current state and not on where you are going in God. People with true discernment are able to see who God has called you to be not when you get there but when you are enduring the trials that are preparing you for the high place.

David's house is spoken of and when David came to fulfill the promise he asked about the house of Saul but he was specifically looking for Jonathan's seed. Jesus Christ the Seed of Abraham came to fulfill the covenant so the families of the earth could be blessed. He was God the Word who became flesh in order to pave the way for us to receive the inheritance. The great commission is a command from Jesus to go into world and make disciples; many of the future disciples are dwelling in a mental state called Lo-debar. Some churches have become a place of comfort instead of a place of healing and sending out. Through the stripes of Jesus God has healed us and brought us out of the low place so we should be willing to tell others of His goodness. It is fascinating that in the root word of the definition of the word pasture are the words friendship, companionship and the word pastor. A person can have all the trappings of wealth but if he does not have companionship or true friendship he will be a very lonely individual. Adam was created by God and had communion and fellowship with God; and God said, *"It is not good that the man should be alone; I will make him an help meet for him Genesis 2:18.* Quiet time alone is good but being in a solitary place alone for long stretches in not good because we were not created to be alone; we were created to have companionship; with God and with others. There are individuals in the body of Christ who feel they do not need to be connected to a pastor and that is a grave mistake. There is a reason why a pastor is one of the gifts given to the saints by Jesus for their edification and perfection.

A pastor stands in Christ stead as a care giver for the sheep—to nurture and bring them to a place of maturity in Him.

The Prophet Jeremiah told the people God would give them pastors after His own heart who would feed them knowledge and understanding; the ensuing result would be they would multiply and increase in the land. Unfortunately many people have a misconception about the pastoral gift and that misconception is based on excesses and indulgences they have witnessed in some areas. Some have been hurt by a pastor and that hurt has sent them into a backslidden state. We must remember where the genuine is, there the counterfeit will reside. We must also remember that pastors are humans and have their frailties and passions like the rest of us.

Not Just a Meal Ticket

David was more than a meal ticket out of Lo-debar for Mephibosheth—he was a shepherd king. When Stephen was before the Elders of Israel, he told them David was a man after God's own heart and he would fulfill all of God's will. David did not roll out of bed and become a man after God's heart, a man to fulfill all the will of God overnight. There was a process of preparation which led him through Lo-debar in the form of wildernesses and strongholds and the cave of Adullam. He had to flee from Saul who was trying to kill him because of jealousy. In the cave of Adullam he had to take care of his father's household when they came to dwell with him.

He reached a point where he was overwhelmed by the repeated attacks of Saul and decided that it was better for him to dwell in the land of the Philistines. When he was given a territory known as Ziklag to dwell, he could not find solace or comfort there because the Amalekites burned it and took all the women and children captive—when that happened the people who were with him threatened to stone him. David had to encourage himself in the Lord his God to survive. What has the spirit of Amalek stolen from you and has it driven you to a place of despair because people close to you are stoning you with their words and their negative attitudes? Don't allow it to trap you in Lo-debar—like David, encourage yourself in the Lord your God.

Chapter 7

---■---

The Good Shepherd

I n the gospel of John Jesus calls Himself the good Shepherd who giveth His life for the sheep. He went on to tell His disciples that He knew His sheep and they knew Him. Jesus was born King so it is safe to say He is the Shepherd King. The only one who can lead a person out of Lo-debar is the Shepherd King. As the King He is sovereign and has the authority and as the Shepherd He has the love and compassion to take the sheep to a peaceful and prosperous place. David was a type of Christ because he was a shepherd first then a king. He had the authority to lead Mephibosheth out of Lo-debar into a place of restoration. Mephibosheth was a type of lost sheep who had been forced into a low place because his feet or his walk was hindered by a life-altering calamity. His walk was messed up because of the nurse's decision and our feet or our walk was messed up because of Adam's decision to rebel against God.

True restoration and redemption comes through King Jesus alone. The Bible confirms this with the scripture, *"Verily, verily, I say unto you, He that entereth not by the door into the sheepfold, but climbeth up some other way, the same is a thief and a robber" John 10:1.* Jesus is the way the truth and the life which leads to the Father so any other way taken will lead to heartache and misery. Jesus is qualified to lead the sheep out of Lo-debar the place of no pasture because He is our good Shepherd and Pastor. He was battered, bruised and beaten severely though He was innocent of all charges; He agonized in the Garden of Gethsemane until His sweat became drops of blood; He endured the low place of the cross for us. When He hung on the cross He experienced everything that would afflict and affect us.

He was despised and rejected, shamed and scorned, forsaken by His own, led like a lamb to the slaughter. He was God in the flesh but he felt the weight of the sins of the world. I was ministering recently and I asked the congregants, which one of them would give their child for a murderer, a rapist, or even a thief and a liar? We would give our lives for the ones we love but not for someone who is a pariah, a person who deserved punishment. According to the scriptures, the good Shepherd gave His life for us when we were in sin. We deserved death because God's righteousness demands that sinners be judged and every one of us was found guilty—the sentence was death but instead of death God not only pardoned us but has blessed us with eternal life through Jesus Christ.

There is not another person who walked this earth who was able to take upon Himself the sins of the world; many have come in the name of religion and many have followed them but were not able to find green pastures because they were not the good Shepherd. Father God allowed Jesus to be dropped so the door could be opened for us to come out of Lo-debar and find pasture and in that pasture we forage with intense hunger, thirst and longing, searching and seeking His presence, comfort, guidance and the voice of the good Shepherd. There is no temptation that is unknown to Him because—according to the scriptures, He was touched with the feelings of our infirmities as our High Priest—He was tempted in all points as we are, yet without sin. He knew no sin but He became sin for us so we could be called the righteousness of God.

Jesus said His sheep hears His voice and He knows them by name. He knows you by name because the relationship you have with Him is very personal. He is not some distant God far out in the cosmos who is unconcerned with the sufferings of His people. When you find yourself in the low place, it can be difficult to hear His voice because your thoughts can succumb to the voice of fear and fear drowns out the still small voice of the Holy Spirit; when that happens the voice of the enemy becomes much more amplified without interference or disruption.

Distrust, apprehension and indecisiveness prevails and overtakes us when we follow a stranger's voice and not the familiar voice of the good Shepherd.

The Good Shepherd

You must shut out all contrary voices and listen intently for the voice of the good Shepherd. His voice will lead you in the direction of green pastures. Any voice that tells you to go in another direction is the voice of the thief and the robber. The thief does not care about the sheep and seeks to destroy them. Jesus declared, "The thief cometh not, but for to steal, and to kill, and to destroy: *I am come that they might have life, and that they might have it more abundantly" John 10:10*. The thief is the devil who only wants to scatter the sheep and has no concern for their welfare, causing them great harm unlike the good Shepherd who gathers the sheep into His protective fold.

The devil is roaming around like a roaring lion seeking whomever he may devour. When David was first summoned to the palace to play for Saul and he found out a Philistine giant named Goliath was tormenting the people, he stepped up to the challenge and prepared himself to defeat the giant. Saul thought David was too young to go into battle against Goliath but David told him, "Thy servant kept his father's sheep, and there came a lion, and a bear, and took a lamb out of the flock: And I went out after him, and smote him, and delivered it out of his mouth: and when he arose against me, I caught him by his beard, and smote him, and slew him. *Thy servant slew both the lion and the bear: and this uncircumcised Philistine shall be as one of them, seeing he hath defied the armies of the living God" 1 Samuel 17:34-36*. The counterfeit lion seeks to pull the lamb out of the flock in order to devour it but King Jesus defeats every giant, every thief and every robber.

The enemy wants to steal your joy and your peace. He wants to cripple your walk with God and leave you in a deplorable and desperate state. Jesus the good Shepherd came to give you life and that more abundantly. There is no abundance or prosperity in Lo-debar; there is no joy or peace there. The sheep should never settle for less, tolerate or accept insufficiency, never settle for anything less than the abundant life. Jesus also described Himself as the door, the gate for the sheep through which a man can enter and be saved.

When Jesus used the word saved, He used a word that means more than fire insurance for salvation and a get out of hell card.

The Greek word for saved is sozo: pronounced sode'-zo; It means to deliver or protect, to heal or to preserve, to do well, be or make whole. Salvation is not a mere religious experience but it is an epiphany, a great awakening and an intense stirring of one's soul of the need to walk out of darkness and out of a blind stupor into a life of living in the glorious and marvelous light of God.

Jesus knows us by name and came to make us whole so we do not have to live broken fragmented lives. Our Shepherd is multi-faceted because He is also the Potter who will put the broken pieces in our lives back together. As previously stated, that is why Jesus asked the lame man at the pool of Bethesda, Will thou be made whole? He did not ask the man if he wanted to be healed because He could have healed the condition but the man would have arose with other issues. The good Shepherd desires to deal with the root issues and not the symptoms. When we are made whole, it means nothing broken, nothing lacking, and nothing out of balance. In salvation there is deliverance, protection; healing, preservation and well-being; when all these components come together and are in sync we are guaranteed wholeness.

Liberation from Lo-debar

If you are reading this from Lo-debar at the present time, a physical or a mental place of despair and depression, please take a moment and talk to the good Shepherd because He knows you personally. Thank Him for His Shalom, His peace which passeth all understanding, the peace that is guarding your heart and your mind. Why does he guard the heart and the mind?—because the issues of life flow out of the heart and as a man thinketh in his heart so is he. The Bible lets us know that the mouth speaks from the abundance of the heart. If there is an abundance of sorrow in the heart negativity will predictably come out of the mouth. That is the reason why the Lord said He will give us a new heart, a heart that is full of love and peace not bitterness, fear and doubt. The Greek word for heart is kardia: it means the thoughts, feelings or the mind. The heart and mind is synonymous; they work in synchrony and harmony with each other. Intellectually we think with our brains but emotionally we reason, feel and act with our hearts and that is why it is often said to take note and listen to your heart.

When a person's arteries are clogged, blood flow is restricted and there is a risk of cardiac arrest or what is commonly called a heart attack. Do not allow the cares and the issues of life to clog your natural and spiritual arteries restricting the flow of the oil of the Holy Ghost; you must allow the peace and love of God to flow out of your heart. Jesus is the greatest heart surgeon and He alone is able to replace the badly broken and abused heart with a new one; *"A new heart also will I give you, and a new spirit will I put within you: and I will take away the stony heart out of your flesh, and I will give you an heart of flesh" Ezekiel 36:26.* Earthly heart surgeons can perform a multiple bypass on your heart to keep the blood flowing or they can transplant someone's heart to the patient but they are unable to give someone a new heart.

A Lamb to the Slaughter

Jesus laid down His life for the sheep and declared that there are other sheep that are not in the fold. The other sheep will distinctly hear His voice and be brought into the fold so there can be one fold and one Shepherd. Unity in the fold is of the utmost importance. There is no room in the body of Christ for us to fragment into the Black church, White church, Latin or Hispanic church, etc. Jesus made it clear in John Chapter 10 that there will be no schism in the sheep fold. There has to be oneness among the sheep. When He spoke those words He was speaking to a predominantly Jewish audience, but He did not limit it to them because He clearly stated that He had other sheep that were not in the fold and they would hear His voice. Some of those sheep are in Lodebar the place of no pasture/pastor and they will hear His voice and will enter His fold and be made whole.

Chapter 8

The Kindness of the King

I was watching Christian Television recently and there was a very prominent minister speaking. She was rebuking Christians for having the audacity to question their pastor. She felt the sheep should not go to certain places unless their pastor gave them permission. She actually called the people dumb sheep. I can understand someone saying a sheep that is an animal can appear not to be very smart, but when the Bible uses the word sheep it is referring to a people who are following and being cared for by Jesus and are totally dependent on the good Shepherd.

The sheep of Jesus' fold are not dumb because they have the Holy Spirit and He gives them wisdom knowledge and understanding. I believe in order and decency in the local church but we are not called to be robots that must be programmed to move. Out of courtesy we should let the leader know where we will be but mature Christians do not need permission from anyone to do what the Lord instructs them to do. We are the Lord's people and the sheep of His pasture and we are not to be controlled by other human beings. Children need permission to go and come because they are not at a place of maturity where they are able to make sound decisions. Immature Christians are like children and need their movements regulated but the mature are led by the Spirit and go whithersoever He sends them.

For the Father's Sake

When David found out that Jonathan had a son that was dwelling in Lo-debar he sought him out. When he came before David he prostrated himself and did reverence.

When David called his name he said, "Behold thy servant!" "And David said unto him, "Fear not:" The first issue David dealt with was the issue which caused his nurse to drop him when she made haste to flee with him upon learning of the death of his grandfather and father. David alleviated any fears he had by telling him, *"for I will surely shew thee kindness for Jonathan thy father's sake, and will restore thee all the land of Saul thy father; and thou shalt eat bread at my table continually" 2 Samuel 9:7.* I love the fact that all follows restoration. The King does not give partial restoration He gives full restoration.

The religions of this world contain partial truths but only King Jesus can give full restoration because He is the whole truth. Mephibosheth is shown kindness by the king for the sake of the father. Kindness from the King leads not only to restoration but to transformation. What a beautiful picture of the type of restoration and transformation received through King Jesus for the Father's sake. He did not and could not have done anything to earn the king's kindness; the kindness flowed from a covenant of love between David and his father Jonathan. It was a covenant of love that manifested grace. That grace represents unmerited favor and divine enablement.

When sin had us trapped in Lo-debar, our freedom and deliverance was secured through a covenant of love. Out of that covenant of love grace was extended to us so we could be redeemed and restored. The only thing we needed to receive the grace was belief which is faith or trust. *"For God so loved the world that He gave His only begotten son that whosoever believeth in Him should not perish, but have everlasting life" John 3:16.* Believeth is one of the key words because without belief a person will not receive the love gift given them by the Father.

David had to deal with Mephibosheth's fear because fear cripples and nullifies faith and trust. A person will not follow someone he does not believe in or trust. There are many remaining static in the land of Lo-debar, constrained to make an effort to put one foot in front of the other there are many immobilized choosing to remain in a paralytic state and unable to break free because they do not believe and therefore they are unable to receive the liberating love God has provided for their freedom.

Although grace is freely available to them, their fear and unbelief blinds them and keeps them from receiving the gift of grace which would restore and redeem them. They are in such darkness they cannot see—the Apostle Paul describes it in this manner, *"But if our gospel be hid, it is hid to them that are lost: In whom the god of this world hath blinded the minds of them which believe not, lest the light of the glorious gospel of Christ, who is the image of God, should shine unto them" 2 Corinthians 4:3-4*. Lo-debar is a dark and dry place but the light of the glorious gospel can shine in the depths of the darkest place in order that the lost can see their way out. Vain religion keeps people trapped in a darkness which appears as a pseudo light. It is a false light that lures the unsuspecting adherents in, binds their minds and controls their actions.

Mephibosheth may have felt threatened because he was the grandson of Saul and David was the one chosen to replace him; David made sure he knew that he was there to bless and not hurt him. David dealt with the fear factor in him because most kings of that day would attempt to wipe out the families of their rivals to prevent any of their descendants from seeking the throne. He did not understand that David was not like most kings, he was the Lord's anointed, a man after God's own heart. The heart of God is kindness and mercy not judgment and condemnation. He takes no delight in the death of the wicked and will only use judgment and implement punishment when his mercy and kindness are rejected.

He was lame in Lo-debar for so long that he did not know who to trust. He lost his grandfather, his father and many other family members at an early age and suffered the crippling injury at an early age. There are people who have experienced a barrage of tragedies that have left them physically and emotionally debilitated. One tragedy can lead to a life of depression and despair and he suffered multiple tragedies. The length of a tragic situation should not cause you to give up and lose faith in God. He controls the events that take place in the times and seasons of your life.

The Lion King

Jesus is our King and He is the conquering Lion of the tribe of Judah; The Lion King defeated the dragon. David was king of Judah and God used him to deliver the Israelites from their enemies. One meeting with the king and Mephibosheth was not only about to come out of Lo-debar but he was about to receive full restoration of the land from his grandfather's estate. One moment he was a prince living like a pauper and the next moment he was in the presence of a great king who came to honor a covenant.

Our fortunes can radically change in the blink of an eye for better or for worse. Our connection to King Jesus and His covenant is an entitlement that He has extended to us all and is the very reason why any low place in which we find ourselves should be looked upon as simply a temporary state equipping us for betterment and greatness and not a permanent place of existence. Mephibosheth was about to go from living meagerly, dependent on the charity, kindness and support of others; from abiding in someone else's home and owning absolutely nothing to becoming an affluent land owner and lord of his very own estate—that news should have led him to rejoice and express unending gratitude to King David but he says something rather peculiar to the king instead. *"And he bowed himself, and said, What is thy servant, that thou shouldest look upon such a dead dog as I am"* 2 Samuel 9:8.

The term dead dog was used by Mephibosheth because it was an accurate depiction and true representation of how he felt on the inside and what is thought and felt by one internally in their heart and mind is inescapably and irrevocably traversed to the outside and is externally reflected for the whole world to see. He genuinely viewed himself as a dead dog. The word of God sheds light on this very thing, *"As water reflects a face, so a man's heart reflects the man" Proverbs 27:19 WET.* Even though he had been born into royalty and his grandfather was crowned a king, he had internalized the most profound shame and inferiority because of his low estate in Lo-debar deeming himself undesirable, unimportant, undeserving and unworthy for recognition and honor before King David.

56

The Kindness of the King

King David could have given Mephibosheth half the kingdom and he still would have responded in the same manner because you can physically take Mephibosheth out of the land of Lo-debar, honor him with a prestigious title and the status of nobility, elevate and position him in the royal palace, clean him up and dress him in royal robes woven from the rarest, finest silk, place a glittering, bejeweled crown on his head and put platinum gold rings on his fingers, lavish him with unimaginable wealth, untold riches and fill his treasures with gold and silver but physically, mentally and emotionally his heart would not be in the right palace. His heart would be elsewhere. It would be located in a low place of impoverishment; in Lo-debar. He could not extricate himself from the denigrating term and projected self-image of feeling and looking like a dead dog and from the subsequent shame and shabbiness of what brought him to Lo-debar in the first place. He needed a mental metamorphosis.

The name Mephibosheth means exterminator of shame. What is your shame? What is keeping you from enjoying an enriched, victorious and abundant life? What is keeping you exiled in a land called Lo-debar? There are people that remain permanently trapped in Lo-debar never moving forward, never making an attempt to seek liberty and refuge to brighter, greener pastures suffering from the shame and abject humiliation of rape and molestation, anguished by the trauma of sexual abuse and perversion or any number of strongholds in one's life. The enemy uses these things to keep them bound. On their own they cannot summon the fortitude, strength or resolve to be released from the fierce clutches of the mentally abusive and tormenting grip. King Jesus is the only one who can exterminate the unceasing shame and feelings of inadequacy delivering and freeing them from any further condemnation.

Shame will cause a person to hide and shun people because they are fearful of exposure. Shame took domination over Mephibosheth's thoughts and low self-esteem set in to shape and defined his life producing self-loathing, self-defeatism and self-sabotage. His years in Lo-debar had taken a severe toll on his mind so the only way he could describe himself to the king was that of a dead dog because he must have felt dehumanized and debased in Lo-debar and stripped of all his dignity, his quality of life and all his rights as a man and most importantly as a viable human being.

He thought of himself as an abased, bestial creature and a dead one at that. Being in a low place had destroyed his self-worth affecting his self-perception chipping away and eroding all of his confidence. Instead of celebrating his elevation out of Lo-debar to a higher place and his restoration and newfound wealth bestowed upon him by the king—he is unemotionally and undeservedly questioning why the king would bother to trifle with him at all.

I was introduced to a young person a while back and I noticed when I spoke to her she did not look me in the eyes. I found out that she previously lived in a home where she was verbally abused to the point where she felt hopeless and unloved. When a person's self-esteem has been trodden down for years it takes a process to get them to the place where they feel they have value. Are you questioning why the King and others are looking at you? If so, please recognize there is a hero within you; a precious jewel waiting to be brought to the forefront. The King and those with a trained eye in the Spirit are able to peer deep beyond the rough to see the beautiful priceless diamond deeply imbedded beneath the surface. Negative words may have been spoken to you and over you to dampen your spirit but you should believe what the Lord and His word says about you and not what is spoken by narrow-minded people with little love in their hearts. You must have confidence in who you are and what the Lord desires to do in and through you.

Chickens, Eagles and Grasshoppers

Paul encourages us to think soberly and not to think of ourselves higher than we ought but that does not mean we should look at ourselves in a worthless manner. When God sent the Israelites to spy out the Promised Land, ten of them came back with an evil report. Any report, any thought, any expression, any interpretation outside of the realm of faith which contradicts, compromises deviates, disputes, or adulterates what God has spoken in His word is an erroneous, negative, evil affirmation. It represents unbelief and unfaithful treachery against God because in essence we are calling God a liar who does not stand in the truth of His word and we defiantly spurn the entrustment and validity of His written oracles.

The Kindness of the King

If God has inspired it, if God has endorsed it, if God has interpreted it, if something has been divinely written with the very finger of God conveying His most personal thoughts, God is under obligation to honor His word. God takes lifeless and inert symbols forming them into words and takes those words and forms them into sounds that when they are spoken brings them into life. His words become infinite, indestructible, immutable, powerful and full of life and by bringing them into existence He orders them to perform authoritative, unlimited, untold action. God has absolute allegiance to His word; if something proceeds out of the very mouth of God, it shall come to pass as confirmed in *Isaiah 55:11*. *"So shall my word be that goeth forth out of my mouth: it shall not return unto me void, but it shall accomplish that which I please, and it shall prosper in the thing whereto I sent it."* We do God a major dishonor and an injustice when we doubt and reject His word. *Numbers 23:19 ESV says, "God is not man, that he should lie, or a son of man, that he should change his mind. Has he said, and will he not do it? Or has he spoken, and will he not fulfill it?"* The answer to all those questions is a resounding YES.

This is what they said to Moses, *"And there we saw the giants, the sons of Anak, which come of the giants: and we were in our own sight as grasshoppers, and so we were in their sight" Numbers 13:33.* Perception is reality for many people and people will treat us according to how we perceive ourselves. The Shunamite woman perceived that Elisha was a holy man of God and she treated him accordingly. The widow of Zarephath saw Elijah as a man of God and treated him accordingly when she made his meal first. The people of Jesus' home town could not receive many miracles from Him because of the way they perceived Him. If you think and act like a chicken people will treat you like a chicken, if you think and act like a grasshopper people will treat you accordingly. Even when you find yourself in the low place, think and act like an eagle preparing to soar.

Despite being in the low place, always reach for, always project, aim, think and perform at your highest caliber, your highest standard with a spirit of excellence. There may be chickens all around with their eyes and their beaks to the ground, there may be grasshoppers all around who think small but do not succumb to their mode of thinking.

IT'S TIME TO COME OUT OF LO-DEBAR

When Ezekiel sat by the river Chebar among the captives he did not act like a captive. He did not spend his time weeping by the rivers of Babylon. He looked to the heavens and saw visions of God. If you are willing to look up from Lo-debar the King will show you a way out.

PART 3:

RESTORED BY THE KING

Chapter 9

——◾——

Mental Metamorphosis

King David took Mephibosheth out of Lo-debar but the real challenge would be to get Lo-debar and all that it represented out of Mephibosheth; to get the low place, the low stature and the low manner of thinking out of his mind. When you entertain thoughts that are averse to the word of God and they become entrenched in your mind it quickly produces a mindset, a type of dogged mentality that is determined to be immovable, unshakable and indelible. You have to constantly renew your mind with the word of God but once a person refuses to surrender their avowed way of thinking it becomes extremely problematic to uproot and redirect them from that particular mindset or mentality. A change of venue, a change of environment, a change of lifestyle, even a change of fortune like Mephibosheth cannot alter the outer man who refuses to alter his inner man and whose thoughts are still stuck and greatly influenced by a place like Lo-debar.

Thoughts affect your attitude and your actions. One of the most difficult mindsets to deal with is a religious mindset because of its rigidity. The Greek word for mind is noema; it means a perception, the intellect, disposition, and thought. It is important to be perceptive where spiritual things are concerned, the Spirit of wisdom and understanding should sharpen your intellect allowing you to think godly thoughts and have a peaceful disposition. You cannot manifest these things if you do not allow the good Shepherd to liberate you from Lo-debar through a mental metamorphosis.

Mental Metamorphosis

When an individual has been indoctrinated with the dogma of a denomination, they will be so tunneled in their minds they stubbornly refuse to see and accept the truth in the scriptures which contradict the rudiments and the traditions of their denomination. The environment a person grows up in and the people of that environment will determine how that person acts and thinks. When an animal has been caged for a long period of time it will function as if it is still caged even when it has been freed; liberation must take place in the mind first then it will manifest in the thought process and the thought process will affect any action undertaken.

There are women who have been in an abusive relationship for such a long time they often suffer from battered woman's syndrome. The person who has never experienced such trauma may ask the question, "Why didn't she just get up and leave?" Once the abuser gets control of the mind through verbal and physical beatings it becomes very difficult for the abused to muster enough courage to flee. Slaves were so severely beaten when they tried to escape their wicked masters, some of them refused to ever make another attempt to escape. Egypt represents a place of bondage and God's people the Israelites spent many years there. Once liberated, they were led through the wilderness for forty years before they could enter the Promised Land.

Many generations grew up in Egypt and developed a certain mindset called slave mentality. Slave mentality means being free physically but mentally remaining bound and under constant captivity, oppression, persecution and subordination to someone or something. Because of slave mentality the Israelites desired to go back to Egypt. They desired to go back to their place of familiarity and under cruel authority of their demanding taskmasters whipping them into position to carry out their orders and purposes. Slave mentality instilled in them a relentless desire to go back to their previous place of laborious drudgery that their former lives afforded them because they were unable to comprehend, cope or fully enjoy their newfound freedom. Although no longer under forced enslavement, they still thought and acted very much like a slave and felt a sense of comfort and security in that state shunning the feeling of empowerment that only emancipation could have brought them in the Promised Land.

Because of slave mentality, murmuring and complaining, discontentment and disobedience they were denied entry to the Promised Land and would never experience, enjoy or eat the good of the land that God had graciously prepared for them because they were still tethered to Egypt.

In the wilderness God called Moses up into the mount to give him Ten Commandments in order to teach the nation how to live with one another and live a life was pleasing to God. Many of them died in the wilderness because they refused to change their attitude and their way of thinking. Many of them actually chided Moses for not allowing them to remain in Egypt to revert back to slaves where they were forced to make bricks without straw. The longer you stay in a place or situation, the more you will adapt mentally and physically to that environment. Stay in Lo-debar long enough and your thinking and your actions will reflect life in Lo-debar no matter where you are.

Negros were freed from slavery many years ago but getting some minds freed from the residual, imaginary chains of mental slavery has been very challenging. The situation is made more difficult when we live in a world where a white skin and straight hair rules and is seen in a much more favorable light than having dark skin and course hair. For many years the Negro people were portrayed in movies and on television as slow-talking, slow-moving and slow-thinking buffoons of entertainment while scoffing, ignoring, obscuring, diminishing, stifling and underutilizing their true talent and exceptional gifting. Having no choice in the matter, they were often cast in parts that would involve acting in minor, demeaning, marginalized, insubstantial roles habitually performing domestic duties that required them to be house servants, maids, cooks, chauffeurs, and field hands just to name a few. Many individuals have paid the ultimate price of sacrificing their lives because of a refusal to continue with the status quo of living in a system where they and their children were relegated and subjugated to second class citizen status.

The N Word

The term nigger was used in a derogatory sense to demean a black person so it was not surprising when many in the community were perplexed and infuriated when the term gained popularity in some segments of the community;

That popularity took place when some rappers began to use it in their songs as a badge of honor. When they used it many of their fans began to use it to describe one another. Control a person's mind and you will control their movement. I believe the people who control the media will control the minds and the movements of the populace. If what you see on television did not affect your thoughts and your actions why would advertisers pay such hefty sums for television commercials, especially during certain sporting events like the Super Bowl?

Racism is institutionalized because it is deeply entrenched in people's minds and people treat others based on their perception of them. One of the residual effects of physical and mental slavery is the entrapment of many of the people of color to accept their fate of deprivation and poverty as the norm that limits their opportunities for advancement and prosperity. There are great opportunities available here in the United States but for some the deck is already stacked against them and they feel genuinely disqualified for a life of success. They become disillusioned, disempowered, disheartened and disenfranchised held captive, imprisoned and constrained by their way of thinking; by Lo-debar mentality.

Break the Chains of Mental Slavery

A stacked deck should never be used as an excuse for failure; it means more hard work has to be put in to achieve the desired goal. Slavery and the Jim Crow system were designed to keep blacks in a low place. I vividly remember an advertisement by the United Negro College Fund which stated, "A mind is a terrible thing to waste." The idea behind it was to encourage education as a way to uplift a people in order to take them out of poverty. An inactive mind is a mind that is being wasted. A wasted mind will consign one to a wasted life and a wasted life is indicative of a nonproductive and ineffectual life that is deemed a worthless life devoid of purposeful aim and intent. Knowledge is power and slaves were forbidden to receive an education because their masters knew if they allowed them to receive an education that education would lead them to strive to elevate themselves. There are individuals who resign themselves to a certain low state for generations.

They build up a tolerance and a comfort level and learn to operate within the confines of the low place, even though it is not conducive to prospering mentally and physically.

Being in a state of agreement to accept life in a low place will always keep one in bondage never experiencing the fullness of life and promotion to a higher place. Most of us have heard of the saying, "If you can change the way a man thinks, you can change the man." *As a Man Thinketh author James Allen (1864–1912)* was a British philosophical writer and he puts the concept of transformational thinking into proper perspective: "Let a man radically alter his thoughts, and he will be astonished at the rapid transformation it will effect in the material conditions in life." Take a look at what he says about failure to achieve success: "All that you accomplish or fail to accomplish with your life is the direct result of your thoughts."

The power to leave Lo-debar, the power to attain success, the power to attain material wealth and all that you desire in life all begins with just one solitary thought. It is never too late to revolutionize your life, never too late to regenerate your mind with the word of God and redirect your destiny by merely changing the way you think and ridding yourself of Lo-debar mentality, dead dog mentality, victim mentality as opposed to Kingdom mentality and receive all that God has laid up for you to bless you in this life when you serve and honor the King in reverential fear.

A great example is a person who has spent many years in prison and eventually becomes acclimated to the prison system and way of life that prison affords them that they subsequently develop a feeling of complacence, safety and security in their presently controlled environment. Isolation leading to familial alienation reinforces a strong sense of belonging and feelings that their only family members and loyal comrades can only be found inside prison. Prison allows them to closely bond with the only family they may know, surrogate imprisoned family members. The prison walls and bars forced them into learning how to survive and thrive in a restricted hostile atmosphere. I have heard of examples of individuals who have received their freedom and commit a crime because they feel they cannot function in society—they were institutionalized by the prison system and felt incapable of functioning once they were set free.

They became adept at weaving their way through the structure of prison so they felt more comfortable at home in prison than beyond the boundaries of prison walls. Freedom meant they would have to take full responsibility for their own welfare in a way they did not have to in prison. For some the responsibility is too great and far too overwhelming so they return to a controlled prison environment because they failed to envision themselves becoming responsible, productive citizens and making a life for themselves once they reenter the free world.

In his letter to the Christians at Rome Paul beseeched them not to be conformed to the system of the world but be transformed by the renewing of their minds. He understood that if they did not experience a mental metamorphosis their actions would continue to reflect the culture of Rome and not the culture of the Kingdom of God. A nonconformist attitude to the world coupled with transformation through mind renewal would allow them to discern the perfect and the acceptable will of the Lord. Association breeds assimilation so once you are associated with certain people and certain places; you will assimilate and adopt the characteristics of the particular people and place. There is a familiar saying that goes like this, "when in Rome do what the Romans do." Not everything done in Rome is suitable for everyone.

The challenge for each of us is always to take the mental high road irrespective of the lowliness of the environment we may find ourselves in. That is not an easy thing to do when you find yourself in a place where there is doom and gloom all around, night and day. Live long enough and you will be dropped by someone. Live long enough and you will experience grief that will cause depression. There are things you will experience that you have no control over. The only control you have is over your response. There are individuals who lose hope and feel that it is better to depart this world than to continue to dwell in the low place—the place where the Sun never seems to shine, the place where it is always dark and cloudy. It takes a strong mind to rise above such a place by having faith in God to believe that tomorrow will be a better day and that eventually, change will come. There are times when change will not come until we take the first step to initiate the change. A depressed mind can lead to a depressed atmosphere.

Have you ever been in a room with a depressed person and you could feel the heaviness in the atmosphere? You can go into some people's homes and feel the heaviness and know there is some type of tension in the life of the occupant; on the other hand you can go into another home and feel the peace dwelling there and that peace tells you a great deal about the occupant of that home. God's people have a peace that the world did not give them and that peace is supposed to be a constant in their lives, even when they are going through hardship. God is an ever present help in the time of trouble. He is your dwelling or your resting place, a shelter in the time of storm.

In Psalm 84 Korah commented on how amiable the tabernacles of the LORD of Hosts are. He used the word tabernacles which mean they are many. Jesus spoke about the many rooms or mansions in His Father's house. Tabernacle is a residence or a dwelling place. One of the Hebrew definitions for the word tabernacle is a shepherd's hut. What a wonderful word to describe the place where weary sheep can find rest in the presence of the good Shepherd. Korah describes Him as "the LORD of Hosts" and it means He fights our battles. He is prepared to battle against anything or anyone who seeks to keep you out of His rest. Korah spoke of his soul longing even fainting for the courts of God. In the tabernacle there was the outer court, the holy place and the holy of holies. The holy of holies represents the third dimension where the presence of God dwells richly and that should be the destination of every Christian.

The psalmist spoke of how blessed the people are who dwell in God's house and how they would continue to praise Him. His house is synonymous with His presence. Lo-debar is the antithesis of His presence and that is why the enemy seeks to keep your mind, soul and body trapped there. He goes on to talk about the people whose strength is in God who when passing through the valley of Baca, make it a well.

According to the Life Application Study Bible published by Tyndale House Publishers, "the pilgrimage to the Temple passed through the barren valley of Baca. No specific valley has been identified, and it may have been symbolic of the times of struggles and tears through which people must pass on their way to meet God.

Growing strong in God's presence is often preceded by our pilgrimage through barren places in our lives. The person who loves to spend time in God's presence will view adverse circumstances as opportunities to experience God's faithfulness and blessing anew. If you are walking through your own valley of Baca today, be sure you are on a pilgrimage toward God, not away from him." When an individual like Mephibosheth, birthed from a royal line but describes himself as a dead dog—it lets us know the severity and the lowliness of his state of mind. He lost all hope and considers his situation as dead and essentially he was a dead man walking in a dead land. Dogs are described as man's best friend because of their loyalty to their masters. To many people dogs are considered part of the family, some of them allow their dogs to lick their faces and some allow their dogs to sleep in their beds. Several years ago some men in the African American community began to refer to themselves and call each other dog. It was not uncommon to hear an individual refer to a close friend by saying, "that's my dog." There was a very popular song out years ago called, "who let the dogs out."

Dogs are not looked upon favorably in the scriptures and at that time were considered unclean animals—I think it is safe to say only pigs are looked upon worse in the scriptures. Jesus declared, *"Give not that which is holy unto the dogs, neither cast ye your pearls before swine, lest they trample them under their feet, and turn again and rend you" Matthew 7:6.* Dog was a term applied to Gentiles by Jews and it was not because Jews considered Gentiles to be their best friends. They believed pagan Gentiles could not receive God's blessing.

Give me a Crumb Lord

Never settle for a crumb when the loaf is available. Matthew records a situation which took place when a Canaanite woman came to Jesus requesting him to have mercy on her daughter who was grievously vexed with a devil—when Jesus did not answer her His disciples asked Him to send her away because they felt she was a bother to them. When it appears that Jesus is not answering your call, do not allow anyone or anything to send you away from Him. Be patient and wait for His response. Jesus told them He was only sent to the lost sheep of Israel. His answer to His disciples made it appear there would be no deliverance for the woman's daughter.

The woman was persistent and asked Jesus to help her. Patience and persistence pays. *"But he answered and said, It is not meet to take the children's bread, and to cast it to dogs" Matthew 15:26.* When He does respond to her His response does not appear to be positive. *"And she said, Truth, Lord: yet the dogs eat of the crumbs which fall from their masters' table" Matthew 15:27.* She never loses her composure throughout the whole process. She was steadfast and firm in her determination to receive from Jesus the deliverance needed by her daughter. Some folks would have gotten an attitude and walked away in a huff about being called a dog missing an opportunity of a lifetime and a miraculous healing.

I remember being a bit perplexed when I first read that verse; I couldn't wrap my mind around the fact that Jesus called her a dog. I would come to understand that He was just reflecting the Jews' attitude of that day which was in stark contrast to His own. Jesus commended her for having great faith when she agreed with Him and told Him, *"yet the dogs eat of the crumbs which fall from their master's table."* She did not spend time debating the dog issue because she knew Jesus only spoke the truth; she told Jesus that the dogs were getting crumbs from their master's table and since she was considered a dog and Jesus was her master, at the very least she deserved some crumbs from Him for her daughter. Her daughter was made whole from that very hour. That woman was one of two individuals Jesus commended for having great faith and both of them were Gentiles. Faith pleases God and it does not matter the ethnicity of the person exercising the faith. When you put your faith in Jesus, He will make you whole.

Elevate your Mind: Free your Soul

Juxtapose Mephibosheth's response to King David when he sought to show him kindness with the response of the woman when Jesus told her, It is not meet to give the children's bread to the dogs. He had completely resigned himself to the low place. His mind's eye would not allow him to see himself as being any better than a dead dog. The king was prepared to restore him to a place of living as a prince but he was trapped in the mindset of a pauper.

71

Mental Metamorphosis

A dog that is full of mange can respond to kindness while it is alive but a dead dog cannot do anything with kindness—the Canaanite woman needed something from King Jesus for her demon-possessed daughter and she was not going to allow anything to stop that. Thought precedes action and when a person's way of thinking is impaired from years of being in a low place, it will affect their actions—attitude determines altitude so you must have an Eagle's attitude in order to soar to an Eagle's altitude!

There are people in society and in the church whose way of thinking is flawed, they do not feel worthy of the kindness the King desires to show them. Expensive costumes, sweet smelling colognes and perfumes are masking the misery they feel from a mind that is trapped in Lo-debar. There are some whose self-worth was destroyed from their childhood because they were constantly told they were nothing and they would amount to nothing. They have dragged feelings of inadequacy and incompetence around for years like an iron ball and chain. No matter how hard they try, they find it impossible to live up to the unrealistic expectations of the mother, father, husband or wife they sought to please but never could. Others continue to suffer from emotional, physical, and verbal abuse for many years in bad marriages and dysfunctional relationships. They have made Lo-debar a habitation and a dwelling place. It is time to soar out of the low place and achieve the greatness you were created to achieve. Leave the heavy baggage of negative thoughts of low self-worth behind. You will not need them on your journey to the King's fully furnished table.

Chapter 10

Rest for a Thirsty Bitter Soul

The 23rd Psalm is a relatively short Psalm but it is loaded with a potent imagery of the good Shepherd, green pastures, still waters, a prepared table, and the restoration of the whole man that vividly displays the goodness and loving kindness of God. David began the Psalm with the emphatic statement; *"the LORD is my Shepherd I shall not want."* He had an excellent understanding of the dynamics of the sheep/shepherd relationship because he spent many hours in the field during his early years tending his father's sheep. When the prophet Samuel came to his father Jesse's house to anoint the new king, David was out tending the sheep. He understood how completely dependent sheep were on the shepherd—without the shepherd they would go astray and be devoured by a predator lying in wait.

Sheep are totally dependent on the shepherd for provision, guidance, and protection. As the sheep of Jesus' pasture you are totally dependent on Him; when you are not submitted to His Lordship you go astray and put yourself in a vulnerable place; that place is where the predator—the devil, roams about seeking whomever he may devour. Failure to obey and follow the voice of Jesus the good Shepherd, failure to submit to the authority of the good Shepherd's written word will cause sin to reign over you and lead you to dry places where there will be lack and want. It is interesting to note—Moses the meek man used by God to deliver His people from the bondage of Egypt spent forty years in the wilderness tending sheep and other livestock. David spent countless hours tending his father's sheep, and Jesus Christ is the ultimate Shepherd of God's pasture.

The sheep will starve to death if the shepherd does not lead them to green pastures. David had a keen understanding of this because he had to lead his father's sheep to green pastures to provide food and rest. He knew that his heavenly Father would take care of his wants as he allowed Him to lead him like he led the sheep. I find the term; *"He maketh me to lie down in green pastures" very fascinating. The Hebrew word for maketh as it is used there is the word, rabats, pronounced, raw-bats'; and it means, make to rest or to crouch on all four legs folded, to recline. The word maketh in English has a connotation of being forced to do something but the Hebrew definition speaks of rest. Remember, Lo-debar means, no pasture.*

When there is no pasture it means water is scarce. Not only did the LORD lead him to green pastures but he led him by still waters—He was led to a peaceful place of no turbulence, just a fertile, lush green place. The Psalm 1 person is compared to a tree planted by rivers of living waters. Because of the kindness of the Lord his Shepherd he would not have to fear evil when he walked through the valley of the shadow of death because he knew the Shepherd was with him. Like David, you must know that your Shepherd will not leave you nor forsake you. There are times where He will allow you to go through wilderness experiences to refine you, teach you, perfect you, and even discipline you. It is during those times when you may feel He is not there and may feel very much alone. It is important in those times to go by what we know and not by what you feel.

In *Psalm 100* he described God's people as the sheep of His pasture. He prefaces that by exhorting the people to make a joyful noise unto the Lord and to serve Him with gladness. It is difficult to be joyful and to serve with gladness when you get dropped and find yourself in Lo-debar. When that happens listen for the voice of the good Shepherd who is able to lead you to green pastures. What happens when you go through a season or time when the pasture is not green and the waters are turbulent? What happens when you get to a place like the Israelites did where the water is bitter? Moses, God's servant led them to a place called Marah and they could not drink because the water was bitter. Marah means bitter; it comes from the root word Mar and it means *bitter, angry, discontented, heavy.*

Everyone can praise and talk about the goodness of the Lord when the pastures are lush and green and the waters are peaceful and calm but in stormy seasons when there is turbulence and where there is nothing but leanness and profound longing in your famished soul because of scarcity, desolation, despondency, will you respond to the adverse hostile environment in an angry, bitter, discontented way? Or will you say like David, *"The LORD is my Shepherd I shall not want."*

Don't call me Mara

The book of Ruth tells the story of Naomi, her daughter in-law Ruth and Boaz the kinsman redeemer. She lived at a time when Israel was ruled by Judges. At that time there was a famine in the land so her husband led the family from their home in Bethlehem to dwell in Moab. Bethlehem means house of bread and Moab was a son of Lot and a byproduct of his incestuous encounter with his daughter. Naomi's husband and two sons died in Moab so she returned to Bethlehem with her daughter in-law Ruth. The upheaval in her life and the loss of her husband and sons caused her to become quite embittered.

When she returned to her home town the people enquired if it was Naomi because she was gone for over ten years. Once they knew it was her they were very excited to see her. Her response to them was, *"Call me not Naomi, call me Mara: for the Almighty hath dealt very bitterly with me"* Ruth 1:20. The name Naomi means the loveable or my delight; years of turbulence left her feeling not so loved and not a delight. She went on to tell the people, *"I went out full, and the Lord hath brought me home again empty: why then call ye me Naomi, seeing the Lord hath testified against me, and the Almighty hath afflicted me?"* Ruth 1:21. She suffered great losses but when she returned home; her daughter-in-law Ruth married Boaz and they both are in the lineage of Jesus. Out of her misery came the greatest minister Jesus Christ. In times of famine and loss of loved ones you can be left with a feeling of emptiness. It is in those times and seasons when you must remember the words of the prophet Isaiah who exhorts us to draw water from the wells of salvation.

IT'S TIME TO COME OUT OF LO-DEBAR

There are times when people blame God for the dry place and the loss they have suffered in life. Jeremiah accused God of deceiving him and prevailing against him because God was stronger than he was. Jeremiah could not handle the fact he was in derision daily and the people constantly mocked him. In Lamentations Chapter Three he describes himself as the man that hath seen affliction by the rod of God's wrath. He accused God of leading him and bringing him into darkness not into light. The constant attacks from a rebellious nation left him in the low place. He said God filled him with bitterness and made him drunk with the wormwood.

His soul was humbled in him when he remembered his affliction, misery, wormwood and the gall. Then he spoke these words, *"This I recall to my mind, therefore have I hope. It is of the Lord's mercies that we are not consumed, because his compassions fail not. They are new every morning: great is thy faithfulness" Lamentations 3:21-23.* It is as if he snapped out of the pity party he was having in the low place by allowing his recall memory to kick in. The Hebrew word for recall is shuwb pronounced shoob; and it means: to turn back or away, to return. He allowed his mind to go back to a certain place and that is what gave him hope. The word for hope is, yachal and it means, to wait; to be patient, to trust.

All of us are in what I call God's waiting room of preparation for divine purpose. The question I ask you the reader is this, "are you waiting with trust and patience or are you waiting with anxiety?" He went back to a place of remembrance and at that place he replaced bitterness and sorrow with patience and trust. The conditions that led him to the low place did not change but his mindset changed because he began to focus on the mercies, compassions and the great faithfulness of God. As bad as things were for him his recall memory took him to a place where he realized, it was because of the Lord's mercies why he was not consumed. He realized that what he was going through did not negate the fact the Lord was merciful, compassionate and faithful.

To the reader who is in a place of feeling empty and bitter at the present time for one reason or another; please do not blame God.

Do not ask, "God why me?" Please do not go by what you feel but go by what you know. For the righteous, the afflictions will be many but comfort can be taken from God's promise to deliver them out of them all. If you are not saved or you turned back from serving Him because of some tragic event—please take a moment right now to repent and ask Him to forgive you of your sins and your trespasses. Repent simply means to turn from where you are to Him; ask Him to cleanse you with the Blood of Jesus and to fill you with His precious Holy Spirit!

Asaph said he knew God was good to Israel but his feet were almost gone and his steps had well nigh slipped when he became envious of the foolish when he saw the prosperity of the wicked. Jeremiah, Asaph and Naomi are just three of many examples of individuals chosen by God who had their moments of weaknesses during difficult times. When you examine the lives of these individuals and what they went through and how God delivered them, it should encourage you to know the Shepherd will lift you out of Lo-debar into green pastures and still waters. Circumstances are ever changing but you can take comfort in the knowledge that the Lord, the good Shepherd will never change. He is the constant in an ever-changing world. People change, places change, things change, and times change but the Lord will always be your Shepherd and you shall not want.

When you place your trust in people and things you set yourself up for major disappointment. I am not suggesting that you should not trust people but the word of God says it is better to put your trust in Him and not your confidence in man *Psalm 118:8*. You should have discernment because people have their inherent weaknesses so engage them with that understanding. The closest people such as a wife, a husband or a blood relative can and will let you down at times but Jesus the good Shepherd, the Lion King can be counted on to be there at all times. According to James, *There is no shadow of turning or variableness in Him.*

The Rod of Wrath or the Rod of Comfort?

In his time of sorrow Jeremiah spoke of the rod of God's wrath.

In *Psalm 23* David said God's rod and staff comforted him. The Jamieson, Fausset and Brown Commentary has this to say about the rod and the staff, *"The "rod" was used by the owner in counting his sheep, which were said, therefore, to 'pass under the rod' Leviticus 27:32.* It cannot refer to the rod of affliction, for here "comfort," not chastening, is what is needed when passing through the darkness. He means, Thy making me to pass under the rod, thereby acknowledging me as thine, comforts me. How many in their dying moments have felt strong consolation in Christ's assurance, *John 10:14, 28-29!* The rod is the assurance which Yahweh gives His child by His Spirit, that He counts him as His own. The "staff" is the emblem of support to the weak. At the same time it is the shepherd's instrument of warding off beasts hostile to the sheep. So *"David took his staff in his hand" in going against Goliath 1 Samuel 17:40;* and the Lord is represented as 'lifting up His staff against' Assyria in behalf of His people Isaiah 10:24. The Word of God is at once a prop to support the child of God, and a defense against Satan and the powers of darkness.

The Good Shepherd Cares for His Sheep

After the death of John the Baptist Jesus got into a ship and went to a desert place. The Greek word for desert as it is used there is the word, eremos and it means, a lonesome or solitary place, a wilderness. The loss of a loved one, the breakup of a marriage or some other tragic event can leave you in a lonely wilderness-like place. As was customary, when the people heard where He was they followed on foot out of different cities. When Jesus saw the great multitude He had compassion on them and healed them. He is so full of love and compassion that he took time out from dealing with the loss of His cousin John to heal others. Tragic events in your life can cause us to shut ourselves up in a dark lonely place, but we should remember that it is out of a place of misery that many ministries are birthed.

Once you can find the inner strength to minister to others while dealing with your own trauma and loss—it will help your healing process. The Lord turned Job's captivity when he prayed for his friends and gave him twice as much as he had previously.

Beloved, can you find a place now in the midst of your situation, in the midst of your lonely desert place to pray for and to minister to someone else? Great testimonies are birthed out of great tests—out of your current test God is birthing a great testimony.

When it was evening the disciples asked Jesus to send the multitude away so they could go into the villages and find food but He challenged them to feed them. Unfortunately they lacked the faith, the finances and the fortitude to get it done. They allowed the immensity of the crowd and the overwhelming prospect of feeding so many mouths due to a lack of resources to determine their response. Fortunately there was a lad there with five barley loaves and two small fishes. *"And Jesus said, Make the men sit down. Now there was much grass in the place. So the men sat down, in number about five thousand. And Jesus took the loaves; and when he had given thanks, he distributed to the disciples, and the disciples to them that were set down; and likewise of the fishes as much as they would. When they were filled, he said unto his disciples, Gather up the fragments that remain, that nothing be lost"* John 6:10-12.

Jesus the good Shepherd had the disciples to direct the people to sit in a place where there was an abundance of green grass. Mephibosheth spent many years in Lo-debar, a place of no pasture, but King David came to lead him to green pastures. True disciples of Jesus will lead thirsty souls to a place of green pasture where there is an abundance of bread and fish—bread represents His presence and fish is symbolic of the soul that is being saved by Jesus. There were five loaves which is symbolic of grace, one of the key ingredients with faith needed for salvation. The number two is symbolic of witness, which is who and what is need to draw souls to Jesus.

The Blood Covenant of Restoration

David told Ziba that he had given Mephibosheth all that pertained to the house of Saul—I love the imagery here because only the King can restore everything to an individual dwelling in Lo-debar, dwelling in the low place of sin. What an awesome image of grace, mercy and love.

King David's kindness to Mephibosheth paints a wonderful picture of the kindness shown by King Jesus when he took the sins of the world upon Himself to restore our walk with God. Sin crippled and destroyed our walk and our relationship with Him but King Jesus went through a process of suffering in order to restore us—ironically, David went through a process of suffering before becoming king over all Israel—before he could gain the kingdom and restore Mephibosheth.

The Hebrew word for restore as it is used there is the word shub, pronounced shoob, and it means to build, to recompense, to recover to refresh or to circumcise. It is interesting that one of the meanings is to circumcise because circumcision was something the Israelites had to do to a newborn son on the eighth day as a sign of the covenant they had with Yahweh. Eight is the number for a new beginning and the covenant Yahweh established with Abraham represented a new beginning for the entire human race. Yahweh told Abraham, *"and in thee shall all families of the earth be blessed" Genesis 12:3.* Several chapters later more of the plan is revealed when Yahweh told him, *"and in thee and in thy seed shall all the families of the earth be blessed" Genesis 28:14.* The Bible gives what is commonly known as progressive revelation. The more of it we read the more is revealed of the revelation of God for us. The Apostle Paul gives an explanation of the Seed in his letter to the Galatians, Now to Abraham and his seed were the promises made. *"He saith not, And to seeds, as of many; but as of one, And to thy seed, which is Christ. And this I say, that the covenant, that was confirmed before of God in Christ, the law, which was four hundred and thirty years after, cannot disannul, that it should make the promise of none effect" Galatians 3:16-17.*

Christ is the Seed and what is the purpose of a seed? The purpose is that it be planted so it can produce fruit. The covenant of restoration was established with Abraham in order to have a people, the Jews, through whom Yahweh could plant the Seed Christ in the earth so gentiles could have their walk restored with Him. The Apostle Paul sheds more light on this when he wrote, *"Christ hath redeemed us from the curse of the law, being made a curse for us:*

for it is written, Cursed is every one that hangeth on a tree: That the blessing of Abraham might come on the Gentiles through Jesus Christ; that we might receive the promise of the Spirit through faith" Galatians 3:13-14.

Another word for covenant is the word testament. Jesus Christ came to give us access to the New Covenant—Testament. The first was based on Law but the second on grace. In order to accomplish that, His blood had to be shed; here is the reason, *"For where a testament is, there must also of necessity be the death of the testator. For a testament is of force after men are dead: otherwise it is of no strength at all while the testator liveth. Whereupon neither the first testament was dedicated without blood" Hebrews 9:15-18.*

When Eve was deceived and Adam sinned, they attempted to cover themselves with fig leaves but Yahweh covered them with the skin of an animal. To get the skin blood had to be shed for their covering. When Yahweh spoke concerning putting enmity between the serpent and the woman's seed, it is what is called the proto evangel. It is the first mention of God's plan to deal with sin and bring restoration to fallen human beings. The manifestation of the seed of the woman would come when Mary gave birth to Jesus. When Yahweh established the covenant with Abraham, He instructed him to, *"Take me an heifer of three years old, and a she goat of three years old, and a ram of three years old, and a turtledove, and a young pigeon And he took unto him all these, and divided them in the midst" Genesis 15:9-10.* The shedding of blood was instrumental in the establishment of the covenant between Yahweh and Abraham.

How does all of that history tie into the covenant between David and Jonathan of which Mephibosheth became the recipient? David did not look for anyone who was left of the house of Saul until the death of Jonathan. While Jonathan was living the covenant could not take effect because he was the legal heir to the throne while he was alive. Salvation did not come while Jesus was alive because His blood had to be shed; His vicarious and atoning death gave force to the covenant Yahweh established with Abraham as it pertained to the gentiles or the families of the earth. Without His death, burial and resurrection, it would not be possible for anyone to come to the King's table to dine continually.

Land for the Seed

When Yahweh appeared to Abram and instructed him to leave his kindred and his father's house—He told him about a land He would show him. In verse seven of the same chapter the conversation moves from land he is to be shown to land that his seed would possess, *"And the Lord appeared unto Abram, and said, Unto thy seed will I give this land: and there builded he an altar unto the Lord, who appeared unto him" Genesis 12:7.* When David found Mephibosheth—after telling him not to fear because he had come to show him kindness, he proceeds to speak about the restoration of land. Land played a prominent role in the covenant Yahweh established with Abraham and land played a prominent role in the covenant David established with Jonathan. When we look at the warfare being waged in the Middle East between the descendants of Abraham—the Jews and the Arabs, the bloodshed is not solely about ethnic and religious doctrine and dogma, but about land. When there is death in a family, the fight for land and other valuable possessions can be lethal.

Mephibosheth was not even living in his own place in Lo-debar, he was in the house of Machir—Maybe it was a blessing that he was not a landowner in Lo-debar; a place of no pasture is not the place to set up permanent residence.

Wholeness in Intellect, Will and Emotions

In *Psalm 23*, the thing that follows the Lord's leading David to green pastures and still waters is the restoration of his soul. The Hebrew word for soul is: *nephesh*, pronounced *neh'-fesh;* it means *a breathing creature*, but it also means vitality. It comes from a root word which means, to be breathed upon or to be refreshed. The years of running from Saul, bearing the responsibility of caring for his father's household when they came to him in the cave of Adullam, the picking up of stones to stone David by the men who had lost their wives and children; the weight of these things would wear down the best of us. In the midst of all that he did not lose sight of that the Lord was his Shepherd. On the other hand, Mephibosheth reached a place where he felt there was no redeemable quality about him. David spoke in Psalm 23 about a table God was preparing before him and he spoke of Mephibosheth dining continually at the King's table.

He refused to feed into his low mental state. When he described himself as a dead dog David called Ziba and told him that he had given Mephibosheth all that pertained to Saul's house.

Down but not Out

Be very careful how you treat a person who is down because you never can tell when the tables might turn. I do not believe Ziba and his family treated Mephibosheth with kindness when he was down in Lo-debar. Ziba would later carry negative news about Mephibosheth to David in an attempt to turn David's heart against him but David honored the covenant he made with Jonathan and could not be dissuaded from restoring Mephibosheth's inheritance back to him. Ziba may not have been happy when David told him that he and his sons and servants would have to till the land for Mephibosheth and bring all the fruits to him. No matter how deep the low place, never give up as long as life is in your body. A reversal of fortune and a major turnaround can occur with just one meeting; a divine appointment; a summons before the King when He extends His golden scepter to summon you forward and gives you unmerited favor as with King David and Mephibosheth. If you are a child of God and have fallen or have been dropped—reach out and take hold of the King's hand and come up higher; come nearer. God told Isaiah that His arm is not shortened that it cannot save.

There are some folks who are happy when you are in Lo-debar but their happiness will be short lived because King Jesus will always honor the covenant. When you sin and the accuser of the brethren tries to bring charges against you—the covenant will always hold, it cannot be revoked or rescinded because it was forged and written in the precious shed blood of Jesus. Make sure you repent of anything that needs to be repented of and know there is no pit that is so deep He cannot pull you out and He is the one who can bring dead things back to life.

Chapter 11

Continually Dining at the King's Table

S ince Mephibosheth was dwelling in the house of Machir, in Lo-debar, his inheritance was unjustly claimed, distributed and enjoyed by others while the rightful heir lived in a low place in Lo-debar with nothing to claim as his own. It took just one encounter with the king to get his inheritance back. You may be the rightful recipient of an inheritance but because of forgery of a will through fraud or greed someone else unscrupulously and undeservedly benefited from your inheritance depriving and stealing it from you. There may be others enjoying a blessing or blessings which belong to you but keep hope alive because a shift is about to take place. You have an inheritance and it does not matter how long it takes, the King will make sure you receive it. Do not allow yourself to die from depression in Lo-debar and forfeit your forthcoming inheritance. When you claim your inheritance it will not be a burden.

The King's Presence and His Presents

Ziba had fifteen sons and twenty servants so there was plenty of manpower to till the land. David kept reiterating to him that Mephibosheth would dine at his table. *"God's blessings maketh rich and adds no sorrow to it" Proverbs 10:22*. Mephibosheth went from no pasture to an abundant harvest. When God restores something you will find it is always better than it was before. While he dined at the table as a son his land would be fruitful because Ziba and company were told by the king to till the land so he would have food to eat. What a great picture of the overflow and overwhelming abundance we get when we are directly connected to the King.

The King's presence truly produces fullness of joy and there are pleasures at His right hand for ever more. Maybe Ziba thought the land would go to him and his sons and the thought of Mephibosheth reclaiming his inheritance was probably the furthest thing from his mind. He may have thought that he had secured the land for himself and his children for generations to come but the word of God states in *Proverbs 20:21 Amplified Version, "An inheritance hast-ily gotten [by greedy, unjust means] at the beginning, in the end it will not be blessed."* Ziba's hope was dashed when he was told they would till the land for Mephibosheth. David told Ziba, *"but Mephibosheth thy master's son shall eat bread always at my table" 2 Samuel 9:10.* Mephibosheth would be sus-tained continually in the king's presence. Without the presence of King Jesus how would we survive?

In the model prayer given by Jesus to His disciples when they asked Him to teach them how to pray—He instructed them to pray, *"Give us this day our daily bread" Matthew 6:11.* Not only natural bread but also the bread of His presence; it was to be requested daily. The natural body can go without physi-cal bread for days, but you need His presence daily; there should be a continual desire for His presence; His word, His touch; outside His presence there is nothing that can truly satisfy. Without His presence there is no fullness of joy. There was a dialogue between Jesus and some people who followed Him be-cause He provided bread that filled their stomachs. He told them not to labor for things that would perish but to labor for the things which He alone could give them, things which led to everlasting life. They inquired of Him what they could do to work the works of God and He responded by telling them to believe in Him. The people were not satisfied with His response so they asked for a sign. Some people find it very difficult to accept that faith in Jesus Christ alone is sufficient for their salvation.

The true Bread from heaven was in their midst but they could not recognize Him because they were stuck in a dispensation when God sent manna from heaven to Moses to feed their ancestors. Get your mind past old things and be-hold the new thing that the Lord has done and continues to do. God told Isaiah that He was doing a new thing but would the people know it?

Jesus told them that Moses did not give them the true bread from heaven. The manna Moses gave them was for temporary sustenance but Jesus the true Bread is everlasting. Once they realized what He was saying they requested that He give them that Bread; *"And Jesus said unto them, I am the bread of life: he that cometh to me shall never hunger; and he that believeth on me shall never thirst" John 6:35*. Jesus' response is further evidence that "Bread" represents His presence because He mentions the word hunger and thirst. Natural bread can fill a hungry stomach but does not quench thirst—the presence of the Lord is spiritual food for the hungry and water for the thirsty soul. The psalmist compared the thirst of his soul for the living God to a deer that panted after the water brook. Jesus is the Water Brook and He invites all thirsty souls to come and drink from the eternal everlasting fountain, HALLELUJAH!!!

"The Showbread" in the tabernacle was also called the bread of His presence because it was to be in God's presence always. It represented a wonderful picture of God's willingness to commune and share with man. The "Showbread" was baked by the priests and they made it with fine flour; twelve loaves were baked to represent the twelve tribes of Israel. The Loaves were to remain on the table before the Lord for seven days—the number seven represents perfection and completion. On the Sabbath the priests would remove the "Bread" and eat them in the Holy Place, and place fresh "Bread" on the table. The Sabbath day represents a day of rest and you can only find true rest in His presence.

The table that the Showbread rested on was made of acacia wood and overlaid with pure Gold just like the Mercy Seat. Wood represents humanity and Gold represents Deity. King Jesus' life represented humanity covered with Deity. The table of "Showbread" was positioned on the right side of the Holy Place next to the lamp stand; The Lamp Stand gave light and is indicative of the fact there is always light in God's presence.

Lame Feet to Beautiful Feet

David's invitation to Mephibosheth to eat bread at the King's table is a wonderful picture of God's invitation to sinners to come and dine at His table continually.

Mephibosheth's lame feet were symbolic of the fact the sinner was not able to walk with God; sin and iniquity caused a breach in the relationship with Adam and God. This breach affected and continues to affect every person born into this world except Jesus because He was born of the Spirit not of the flesh.

Prior to the fall, the Voice of God walked and talked with Adam and Eve in the Garden but that changed afterwards. "And they heard the voice of the Lord God walking in the garden in the cool of the day: and Adam and his wife hid themselves from the presence of the Lord God amongst the trees of the garden. And the Lord God called unto Adam, and said unto him, *Where art thou" Genesis 3:8-9?* In the presence of the earthly king Mephibosheth bowed his face to the ground and questioned why the king would look upon a dead dog such as him. When Jesus' disciples had toiled all night on a particular fishing trip and caught no fish, Jesus instructed them to cast their nets on the other side. Their obedience to His word brought so many fish into the boat that it almost sank. *When Peter saw the overflow, "he fell down at Jesus' knees, saying, Depart from me; for I am a sinful man, O Lord" Luke 5:8.* In the presence of the King of Kings when His awesome power is displayed a true disciple will recognize his or her weakness and frailty.

Adam and Eve tried to hide their weakness when they sinned, prompting God to ask them a rhetorical question. The question was asked to get to the heart of their condition not their location because God is Omniscient and He knew their location and their condition. My experience of being incarcerated in prison in England taught me that sin will take us farther than we want to go, keep us longer than we want to stay and cost us more than we are willing to pay. His question was a call to them to examine themselves and to look at the state that deception and rebellion had placed them in. Let us endeavor to take an honest look and self-assessment at our walk with God and ask ourselves the question, is there broken fellowship? If there is then restoration comes through repentance.

When David first inquired of the whereabouts of anyone left of the house of Saul, Ziba told him Jonathan's son was lame in both feet, our Father in heaven does not need anyone to tell him our whereabouts or our condition because He knows all about us, just like He knew all about Adam and Eve despite their futile attempts to hide their nakedness from Him.

Rags to Riches

Going from Lo-debar to dining at the King's table continually is like going from rags to riches. Something very improbable happened in Mephibosheth's life. He went from being born into a royal family to rags while he dwelt in Lo-debar then back to riches again when he dined at the King David's table. An encounter with the King will transform a person's life permanently if they stay connected to Him. Once a sinner encounters King Jesus and is willing to repent, he or she can be cleansed and brought out of the pit of Lo-debar to have a perpetual feast at His table. Jesus has called every redeem believer to go down to Lo-debar and present the gospel to people dwelling there so they can be liberated. Jesus came for us, David went for Mephibosheth and we must go for others. There are many who have fame, fortune and prestige but no joy nor peace because there is no walk, no relationship with God.

Now are we The Sons of God

When Mephibosheth was brought to the king's table he was not brought there as a peasant or pauper but as a son; David told Ziba that Mephibosheth would eat at his table as one of the King's sons; this is a beautiful picture of the spirit of adoption. The covenant provided a place for Him at the king's table. The son of a king is a prince; what a wonderful picture of restoration. As a king's son he was entitled to all the rights and privileges associated with such a lofty and prestigious position. The position of a son is a most honorable position. Mephibosheth was born a blueblood, an aristocrat with a royal title but when he was dropped his luxurious lifestyle and noble legacy crumbled along with the kingdom of his grandfather King Saul. To worsen matters he became lame in his feet—he wound up as a commoner abdicating physically, spiritually and emotionally to a low place in Lo-debar suffering from an identity crisis, a crisis that caused him to modify his way of thinking and caused his thoughts to be mastered and governed by his severe bodily deformity and unfavorable hostile environment in Lo-debar and to look at himself in a self-deprecating manner so that he thought of himself in the same category as a four-legged animal.

There are many sons of the King who belong to the Kingdom who do not know the truth about their identity and are completely shrouded from finding the truth. Tolerant and submissive to abiding in a low place and reduced to living like a peasant and pauper they settle into living well below their means. They settle for living well below their status, and heritage of what God has bequeathed to His children, His heirs when all that is needed is a change of identity, a change of heart, a change of mentality leading to a complete change of destiny to make them realize the Kingdom of God is readily accessible, the Kingdom of God is beckoning, the Kingdom of God is advancing, and the Kingdom of God is awaiting. The word of God affirms our noble kinship with God, *"The Spirit itself beareth witness with our spirit, that we are the children of God: And if children, then heirs; heirs of God, and joint-heirs with Christ; if so be that we suffer with him, that we may be also glorified together" Romans 8:16-17.*

Our good and most gracious Benefactor wants us to receive our goodly inheritance and go and possess the land but first we must allow King Jesus to rule and reign supremely and sovereignly in our hearts and overthrow the worldly kingdom deposing the prince of this world. We must kneel to Him who sits on the throne and declare our loyalty in abject submission to the one true King, our Lord and Master, our Savior—our King Jesus. God is waiting for us to lay claim to His covenant, God is waiting for us to claim our just portion, God is waiting for us to possess all that He has granted to us long ago by the death and resurrection of His royal Son who will entitle us to a position in the Kingdom of God as royal Kings and Priests.

Revelation 1:5-6 Amplified Version states, "And from Jesus Christ the faithful and trustworthy Witness, the Firstborn of the dead [first to be brought back to life] and the Prince (Ruler) of the kings of the earth. To Him Who ever loves us and has once [for all] loosed and freed us from our sins by shedding His own blood, And formed us into a kingdom (a royal race), priests to His God and Father, to Him be the glory and the power and the majesty and the dominion through-out the ages and forever and ever Amen (so be it)." It is imperative that you allow the King to use you as a vessel to transport His sons out of Lo-debar so they too may occupy their rightful place of honor to sit at His table and never again settle for eating crumbs. One of the names the Spirit gave Peter to call His redeemed people is, "a royal priesthood." People in royal families normally associated with other royals or individuals of stature. We become members of the royal family of Jesus Christ through His nobility and royal blood and through the marriage supper of the Lamb which will take place in the future.

The spirit of adoption has translated us from being paltry paupers to becoming stately princes. The spirit of adoption takes our relationship of kinship with God to a new and higher level. Adoption by the Father has opened the eyes of many to reveal the truth of who they belong to—bona-fide members of the family of God. Once a stray and bewildered sheep but now tenderly embraced and wholly accepted into the fold of the good Shepherd. His precious lambs have been wounded, bruised, broken, lame and blinded by the evil works of the devil effectively shielding their hearts and eyes from knowing the truth; that God is indeed our Father. By our intimate association and close familiarity with Him as sons of God He generously offers us a life that is prosperous, blessed, highly favored and greatly privileged beyond comprehensible measure. Mephibosheth did not come to the king's table as a charity case because he was born a prince. Mephibosheth would have the full rights and privileges of Son-ship. Because of his royal birth he was reinstated to his rightful position by King David honoring his covenant to the royal heir of Jonathan. He had never lost his royal rank or title, only his position in the kingdom when he was exiled to Lo-debar by the death of his father and grandfather. The fact that Mephibosheth lost his inheritance and vast fortune as a member of royalty never negated his title of aristocratic peerage.

Jesus Christ was born a Son, He was born a King but His first resting place was not in a palace but in very humble surroundings born in a stable and placed in a manger used to feed animals. Although He was born a Son, the Bible lets us know that He learned obedience through the things which He suffered.

Reader, you may have come into this world through humble beginnings and may have endured or we may be enduring a time and a season of suffering— your suffering is teaching you obedience and your obedience will bring you into a place of maturity in Him.

God allowed Jesus' beginnings to be humble so those in the lowest of places could identify with Him. The Apostle Paul told the Galatians, *"But when the fulness of the time was come, God sent forth his Son, made of a woman, made under the law, To redeem them that were under the law,* that we might receive *the adoption of sons. And because ye are sons, God hath sent forth the Spirit of his Son into your hearts, crying, Abba, Father. Wherefore thou art no more a servant, but a son; and if a son, then an heir of God through Christ"* Galatians 4:4-7. Paul is not implying that we should not be servants anymore because we should always have a heart to serve but should recognize that we serve as Sons. Sons because Jesus said the servant knoweth not his master's business.

Chapter 12

Complete Restoration

When Mephibosheth sat at the table of King David, his lame crippled feet were hidden under the table. While you are in your earthly body you will deal with crippling and binding issues that you bring to the table that you prefer to have tucked away and hidden in your heart never to be exposed or addressed. Unresolved issues are problematic and serve no purpose other than to obstruct your ingestion of all the good things God has prepared for you to eat in this life. God has set a bountiful table before you and you shall eat in plenty and be satisfied; engorging and delighting yourself with the delectable word of God when you cast all your cares, upon Him.

We came to Christ from various walks of life and various experiences. We all came weighted down with excess baggage which affected us mentally, emotionally and physically. Unfortunately some of us, instead of being delivered picked up more baggage in the church from being dropped or mishandled by others. When we are connected to true spiritual covering—they must be compassionate enough to see us greater than where we are. They must see us greater than we see ourselves. They must see the Diamond in the Rough and be willing to walk us through any and all things which seek to debilitate our walk with God by keeping us in Lo-debar. A Christ-like earthly covering can facilitate growth and development but a wolf masquerading in sheep's clothing will stunt a person's growth and can cause a great deal of harm.

While earthly coverings are ordained and anointed to get us to a place of maturity only Jesus the good Shepherd can take us to a place of sinless perfection. Remember, the good Shepherd leads the sheep to green pastures.

Complete Restoration

Covering should not be used as a façade for absolute control and shearing the sheep to maintain the covering's lifestyle. In the word restoration there are the words, rest and restore. The last Adam Jesus Christ came to restore mankind to a previous place of sinless perfection enjoyed by our fore parents Adam and Eve. Disciples find perfect peace and rest in Christ alone; the religions of this world offer an outward appearance of spirituality, peace and rest but inwardly they are in turmoil basing their religion on performance of works and not grace.

When you sit at the table of the King of Kings there will be no lameness in your feet because they will be completely restored and made whole. You will not get to His table overnight because it is a process filled with fiery trials and temptations. The process began when you confessed and believed in Jesus' vicarious and atoning death, burial and resurrection for your redemption and restoration. Prior to coming to a place of repentance for salvation you were controlled by the lust of the flesh, the lust of the eyes and the pride of life. When you came to Jesus Christ in a posture of repentance a new creature was birthed. The Apostle John declared, *"Beloved, now are we the sons of God, and it doth not yet appear what we shall be: but we know that, when he shall appear, we shall be like him; for we shall see him as he is" 1 John 3:2.* You will not be a Son at a later date because the process of being a son started at the point of salvation through the spirit of adoption which allows you to call God Abba Father which is a term reserved exclusively for His born-again children. The term Son is used generically to encompass both males and females.

Although you are a Son now, the fullness of Christ is not manifested in you because the sanctification process which will lead to glorification will occur when He shall appear. It is what the Apostle Paul refers to when he wrote to the Ephesians about the perfecting of the saints for the work of the ministry. It is the ministry of reconciliation whereby we stand in Christ's stead beseeching and calling sinners to repentance. He has not restored your walk for you to have a lot of style and no substance. Your walk was not restored for you to be a part of exclusive religious meetings with the converted. He has restored it so you can carry the gospel of peace to those spiritually dead and dying who are inescapably bound and defeated in Lo-debar with all its trappings and pitfalls. *"For whosoever shall call upon the name of the Lord shall be saved.*

How then shall they call on him in whom they have not believed? and how shall they believe in him of whom they have not heard? and how shall they hear without a preacher? And how shall they preach, except they be sent? as it is written, How beautiful are the feet of them that preach the gospel of peace, and bring glad tidings of good things" Romans 10:13-15.

Restored feet are beautiful feet because they carry the gospel of peace in a world of unrest. Sons are greatly appreciative of the deliverance King Jesus has secured and the place at the table He has prepared. This is the sole motivation for ministry, not vain self-promotion or self-serving motives which does not bring Him glory. Sons are cognizant of the fact they did not get to the table via human intellect, good looks or fame and fortune. Mercy and Grace those beautiful twins facilitate a place at the table. There will be no one at the table who is not clothed in humility and the robe of righteousness possessing a heart to earnestly serve others unselfishly. You will be refused a seat at the table if you are full of pride and arrogance. There is no place at the table for people who are unwilling to forgive others their trespasses, there is no opportunity to even think of approaching the table with bitterness, resentment, guile, heaviness, vindictiveness, anger and wrath—no place for people who do not have the heart of God the Father which was manifested by Jesus Christ.

In the midst of the severest storm, the people around you should feel the peace and calm coming from you. Old friends and acquaintances should clearly see the before and after picture as far as your restoration is concerned. They will not see perfection because it has not been attained yet but they should witness that you are no longer the person you used to be. When they see a wart or a blemish here and there, they should know they will not last because you are on the path of complete restoration.

Your Children and Your Children's Children

The word of God states, *"A good man leaveth an inheritance to his children's children: and the wealth of the sinner is laid up for the just" Proverbs 13:22.* Mephibosheth had a son named Micha; there is not much information on him in the Bible but you can surmise that he was not able to do much for his son while he lived in the house of Machir in Lo-debar.

While he was in Lo-debar his inheritance was held up and if he was not in control of it ultimately he had nothing to pass on to his son. Once King David found him and began the restoration process his life was transformed and this positioned his son for elevation and a life of prosperity that would extend to his son's posterity and for generations to come.

The great thing about a covenant is that it makes provision not only for the one it is established with but with their descendants. God's covenant with Abraham meant his descendants would continue to benefit from it long after he was gone. The blessing of the covenant was extended to Isaac and when a famine hit the land God instructed him where to dwell and blessed him in that place. He informed Isaac that He was blessing him because of his father's obedience. When Peter preached the first sermon on the day of Pentecost, he told the devout Jews listening, *"For the promise is unto you, and to your children, and to all that are afar off, even as many as the Lord our God shall call" Acts 2:39.* The elevation to the king's table and the restoration of the inheritance meant the despair and the poverty of Lo-debar would not continue to affect Micha and the descendants who would come from his line if he had a child or children.

The Place and the Foundation of Peace

King David's palace was located at Jerusalem proving to be a land of plenty, permanency and stability for Mephibosheth in stark contrast to Lo-debar being a land of desolation with no pasture where his life had no firm foundation after being displaced. Jerusalem means place of peace or foundation of peace. Lo-debar is a place of despair and there is no peace of mind there. Dining at the king's table meant he had a new foundation and it was one of peace. When he sat at that table he did not look upon himself as a dead dog any longer but as a son of the king. Remember, association breeds assimilation so his outlook on life changed because his environment changed. There are times in life when you have to make up your mind that the place you are living in and the people you are surrounded by are not conducive to growth and development. Once that realization comes, be willing to do what is necessary to leave and disassociate with the familiar in order to embrace the promise.

Abram had to leave his country and his kindred and go to a land God would show him. He had to be willing to sacrifice his beloved Isaac when he was tested by God. In order to get to the King's table it is necessary to leave some familiar people, places and things behind. It is not an easy thing to do because soul ties develop over time which causes and attachment to those people, places and things.

In order to get to Jerusalem the place of peace, he had to be ready and willing to come out of Lo-debar. In order to sit in the palace at the king's table he had to get rid of the dead dog mentality and see himself as a son deserving of his inheritance and his position in the kingdom. Beloved, there is a place set at the table for you but you have to make up your mind that you will no longer dwell in the low place. *"Rise up, my love, my fair one, and come away" Solomon 2:10.* Rise up and come away with King Jesus. No longer will you allow your mouth to speak of yourself in a manner that is not befitting or representative of the life of a child of a king. Get ready for your restoration; get ready for your transformation and the receiving of your inheritance.

Like Mephibosheth your deliverance out of Lo-debar has come through the covenant with the King. God will set you in a wealthy place strategically placing you alongside royalty like Mephibosheth who descended to the lowest place and ranks, a disadvantaged outcast in Lo-debar only to find himself ascending to the highest place and position, with an open invitation to sit at the king's table in the royal palace. It was a veritable place of honor; a place of elevation; a place of favor, a place of constant provision and abundance. He was now dining sumptuously every day being served a seven-course meal of rich dainties and savory meats at the king's table.

Life had become a continual feast and banquet but it must have been an inconceivable and unattainable vision in the low places of Mephibosheth's mind to ever envision actually eating at the king's table when he was relegated to living a sub-standard life in Lo-debar eating only crumbs. Ah, but what a difference one day can make. What a major difference a mere 24 hours can do to turn the tables, flip the script, do an about-face, to transform a life out of abject circumstances, out of physical, mental and spiritual impoverishment when God restores you, miraculously feeds you to manifest His glory.

"O taste and see that the LORD is good" Psalm 34:8.

Mephibosheth's exit from Lo-debar was a day unlike any other day, it was a day set apart for a miracle from God. He had nothing but troubles in his life. Lo-debar represented a ghostly landscape of gloom and doom, misery and affliction, discontentment and dishonor until King David came seeking an heir of Jonathan to bless. Where ever you are today, know that there was a covenant established by God and came into force with the shedding of the blood of Jesus. The covenant contains spiritual and natural blessings for you and your family so rise up and receive your blessings because: **IT'S TIME TO COME OUT OF LO-DEBAR!!!**

Additional Books I Have Authored That Will Bless You

Mercy And The Sufficiency Of Grace

Perceive And Receive

Don't Birth An Ishmael In the Waiting Room

From The Pit To The Prison To The Palace

Midnight

Diamond In The Rough

Praise Worship And The Spirit Of Prophecy

The Power Of Persistent Prayer

You can contact the ministry by going to www.fideldonaldson.org

www.ingramcontent.com/pod-product-compliance
Lightning Source LLC
Chambersburg PA
CBHW021241090426
42740CB00006B/641